MEAP
Preparation
and Practice

Level 2

Workbook

A Division of The McGraw·Hill Companies

Columbus, Ohio

Art and Photo Credits: © 2002 www.arttoday.com

www.sra4kids.com

SRA/McGraw-Hill

A Division of The McGraw·Hill Companies

Send all inquiries to:
SRA/McGraw-Hill
8787 Orion Place
Columbus, OH 43240-4027

Printed in the United States of America.

ISBN 0-07-600296-9

 3 4 5 6 7 8 9 MAL 08 07 06 05 04

Table of Contents

MEAP Integrated English/Language Arts Rubric . . . 4

Revising and Editing Checklist 6

Unit 1 Practice Test 8
Unit 1 Test 27

Unit 2 Practice Test 42
Unit 2 Test 61

Unit 3 Practice Test 76
Unit 3 Test 95

Unit 4 Practice Test 110
Unit 4 Test 129

Unit 5 Practice Test 144
Unit 5 Test 163

Unit 6 Practice Test 178
Unit 6 Test 197

MEAP Integrated English/

Characteristics	6	5
Content and Ideas	The writing is exceptionally engaging, clear, and focused. Ideas and content are thoroughly developed with relevant details and examples where appropriate.	The writing is engaging, clear, and focused. Ideas and content are well developed with relevant details and examples where appropriate.
Organization	The writer's control over organization and the connections between ideas move the reader smoothly and naturally through the text.	The writer's control over organization and the connections between ideas effectively move the reader through the text.
Style and Voice	The writer shows a mature command of language including precise word choice that results in a compelling piece of writing.	The writer shows a command of language including precise word choice.
Conventions	Tight control over language use and mastery of writing conventions contribute to the effect of the response.	The language is well controlled, and occasional lapses in writing conventions are hardly noticeable.

Not ratable if:
- off topic
- illegible
- written in a language other than English
- refused to respond

Language Arts Rubric

4	3	2	1
The writing is generally clear and focused. Ideas and content are developed with relevant details and examples where appropriate, although there may be some unevenness.	The writing is somewhat clear and focused. Ideas and content are developed with limited or partially successful use of examples and details.	The writing is only occasionally clear and focused. Ideas and content are underdeveloped.	The writing is generally unclear and unfocused. Ideas and content are not developed or connected.
The response is generally coherent, and its organization is functional.	There is evidence of an organizational structure, but it may be artificial or ineffective.	There is little evidence of organizational structure.	There is no noticeable organizational structure.
The writer's command of language, including word choice, supports meaning.	Vocabulary is basic.	Vocabulary is limited.	Vocabulary is very limited.
Lapses in writing conventions are not distracting.	Incomplete mastery of writing conventions and language use interferes with meaning some of the time.	Limited control over writing conventions makes the writing difficult to understand.	Lack of control over writing conventions makes the writing difficult to understand.

REVISING AND EDITING CHECKLIST

Use the following checklists as you revise and proofread your draft. When you are finished revising, make a final copy of your paper. Then, proofread your final copy to make sure all of your revisions have been made.

CHECKLIST FOR REVISION
- Do I have a clear central idea that connects to the theme?
- Do I stay focused on the theme?
- Do I support my central idea with important details or examples?
- Do I need to take out details or examples that DO NOT support my central idea?
- Is my writing organized and complete?
- Do I use a variety of words, phrases, and sentences?

CHECKLIST FOR EDITING
- Have I checked and corrected my spelling to help readers understand my writing?
- Have I checked and corrected my punctuation and capitalization to help readers understand my writing?

CHECKLIST FOR PROOFREADING
- Is my final copy just the way I want it?
- Does each sentence begin with a capital letter and end with correct punctuation?
- Are there any sentence fragments or run-on sentences?
- Are there any misspelled words?
- Are paragraphs indented?
- Can very long paragraphs be broken into two paragraphs?
- Can very short paragraphs be combined into one paragraph?

MEAP
Preparation
and Practice

Level 2

PART 1: WRITING FROM KNOWLEDGE AND EXPERIENCE

This test is divided into two parts that are linked to one theme or important idea. The theme for this unit is **Sharing Stories.** Refer to the Theme Connections pages at the end of each selection in Unit 1 in your Student Anthology for additional information about the theme. Keep the theme in mind as you are taking this test.

In Part 1, there will be a number of ways to write about the theme. You must choose ONLY ONE way. After you have finished reading the information provided, begin writing a DRAFT. When you have completed your draft, use the REVISING AND EDITING CHECKLIST on page 6 in this workbook to review your writing. Then enter your final copy on the page marked FINAL COPY. You may use a dictionary, thesaurus, grammar book, or spelling book for Part 1 writing.

Tips for Traits of Good Writing
Getting Ideas

For more information on the traits of good writing, turn to page 12 in the *Open Court Reading Language Arts Handbook.*

Before you can start to write a story, you need to have some ideas. The main idea is where you start.

Brainstorming is a way to get lots of ideas. Think of as many ideas as you can. Write them all down. Keep thinking and writing down ideas until you cannot think of any more.

After you have written down your ideas, start crossing out the ones that do not interest you. Then cross out any ideas that do not fit the assignment. Put the ideas you have left into a list.

Use your favorite idea from the list as your main idea in a web. A web is a kind of graphic organizer. You can gather and organize your ideas in a web. Here's how to create one. Start by drawing a small square in the center of the page. Write your main idea inside the square. Think of words or phrases about the main idea. Write them around your center square. These will be your supporting ideas. Put each word or phrase in a square. Connect them to the main idea square. Look on the next page for an example of a web.

GO ON.

The following paragraph was written by Charlie. He decided to share a story about his dog. Notice how the main idea *my dog Trouble* is supported by ideas from the web.

My dog's name is Trouble. He is white with black and brown spots. Trouble chases rabbits in our yard. He chews things up. He barks at the neighbors. He does make a lot of trouble, but he is my best friend.

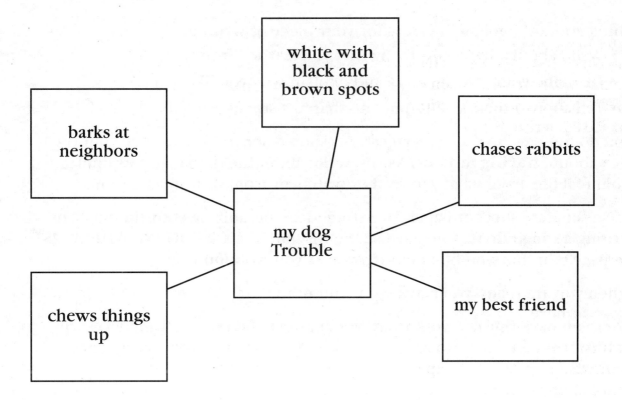

GO ON.

WRITE ABOUT THE THEME: Sharing Stories

Everyone likes a good story. We like hearing them and sharing them with others. Stories allow us to step out of our world for a while and into the world of the story. Some stories are very old. They have been retold and shared for a long time. Other stories are new. Your favorite authors may have written some of them. People share stories for many reasons. Some stories are funny. Others are exciting or mysterious. A very special story may be all these things at once.

Think about the following ideas for your piece of writing:

- Write about a lesson for living that you learned from a story.

- Describe your favorite story and explain why you like it.

- Tell about a time when someone shared a story with you.

You do not have to use the suggestions shown above. You can use your own idea about **Sharing Stories.** As you write about the theme, use examples from real life, from what you read or watch, or from your imagination.

Use a separate sheet of paper for listing ideas, organizing your thoughts, or writing a rough draft. You may use the REVISING AND EDITING CHECKLIST on page 6 in this workbook to help you as you work on your draft.

When you are ready, you may begin your draft.

After you have finished your draft, you may use the English/Language Arts Rubric chart on pages 4 and 5 in this workbook to help you as you write your final copy.

GO ON.

Name _____ Date _____

FINAL COPY

Use the English/Language Arts Rubric chart on pages 4 and 5 in this workbook to check your writing and make changes.

_____

_____

_____

_____

_____

_____

_____

_____

_____

_____

_____

_____

_____

STOP.

PART 2: READING

Tips for Using Context Clues to Answer Multiple-Choice Questions

Some tests have multiple-choice questions. You can use context clues to find the right answer. Read the article below and the question that follows.

> A starfish doesn't always have to look like a star. It can rearrange its arms any way it pleases. This ability allows a starfish to wedge itself into a small place and stay out of sight.

1. Read this sentence in the paragraph: **This ability allows a starfish to wedge itself into a small place and stay out of sight.** What does the word *wedge* mean in this sentence?
   A. spread out
   B. squeeze into
   C. stick to
   D. spill out of

To answer this question, use the surrounding sentences or context clues to help you decide on the best answer.

- In the last sentence of the paragraph, you find the words *into a small space.* Using this clue, you know that the starfish is not trying to spread out. You can eliminate, or get rid of, answer A.

- In the last sentence of the paragraph, you find the words *stay out of sight.* Using this clue you can rule out answer D. The starfish is trying to hide rather than be seen.

- That leaves choices B and C. In the second sentence of the paragraph, you find the words *can rearrange its arms any way it pleases.* That means that it can make itself longer and thinner. This ability would allow it to get into a smaller space. It would not make the starfish stick to anything. Now you can eliminate answer C. That leaves answer B, the correct answer.

Remember to use context clues as you read the following selections and answer the multiple-choice questions that go with them.

GO ON.

DIRECTIONS

Read Selection 1. Answer the five multiple-choice questions that follow Selection 1. You may look back at the selection at any time.

Go on to Selection 2. Answer the five multiple-choice questions that follow Selection 2. You may look back at the selection at any time.

Then answer the two multiple-choice questions in the section called PART 2: CROSS-TEXT QUESTIONS.

As you answer the multiple-choice questions, choose the BEST answer. Do not worry if there are questions you cannot answer. Take your time and do as well as you can.

When you have finished reading the selections and answering all of the questions, you may wish to go back and check your work. Do not go on to the next section until you are told to do so.

GO ON.

Special Saturday

1 Saturday nights were special at Beth's house. Dad and Ben always cooked hamburgers. Mom and Beth made milkshakes. Everyone helped clean up after dinner. Then it was story time.

2 Story time was Beth's favorite time. The family chose a book to read. Every Saturday they took turns reading a chapter. They read all kinds of books. Beth loved them all. But Beth only listened to the stories. She didn't know how to read. This year she was learning to read in school. Tonight she had a surprise for the family.

3 Everyone sat in the living room. Dad pulled the book from the bookshelf and began. It was a story about knights and castles. Beth was so excited she could hardly listen. Soon Dad finished his chapter.

4   "Who wants to read next?" he asked. He looked at Ben and Mom.

5   "I do!" Beth said.

6   Everyone was surprised. "You have never read before," Ben said.

7   "I'm learning in school," Beth said. "I can read!"

8   "Let her try," Mom said with a smile. Dad handed Beth the book.

9   Beth looked at all the words on the page. There were so many! She took a deep breath. Then she started reading.

10   Beth read five pages all by herself. When she finished, her family clapped and cheered. "Good for Beth!" Dad said.

GO ON.

Name _____ Date _____

PART 2: READING SELECTION #1

DIRECTIONS: For each question, circle the BEST answer. You may look back at the selection as often as necessary.

1 Beth hardly listens while Dad reads because she is

A. bored.

B. excited.

C. tired.

D. hungry.

2 Which of these is NOT a reason Saturday nights are special?

A. reading together

B. making hamburgers

C. staying up late

D. making milkshakes

3 What will Beth probably do for the next story time?

A. clean up the kitchen

B. pick a movie to watch

C. ask to read a book

D. dust off the bookshelf

GO ON.

Name _____   Date _____

4 Look at the chart below. It shows the order in which some events happen in the story.

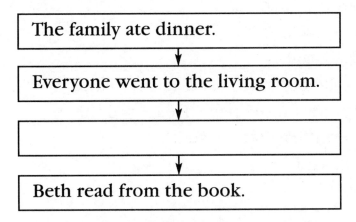

| The family ate dinner. |
| Everyone went to the living room. |
| |
| Beth read from the book. |

Which of these belongs in the empty box?

A. Dad took a book off the shelf.

B. The family washed their dishes.

C. Ben read from the book.

D. Beth learned how to read.

5 Which sentence from the story shows that Beth's family is proud of her?

A. Every Saturday they took turns reading a chapter.

B. Everyone was surprised.

C. Beth read five pages all by herself.

D. When she finished, her family clapped and cheered.

GO ON.

Jackson Reads

1 Jackson was learning to read in school. Every night he tried to read to his mom and dad. But the words were hard. Jackson was ready to give up.

2 "Reading is too hard!" Jackson said.

3 "You can do it," Mom said.

4 "Try again, Son," Dad said.

5 Jackson picked up the book. He tried again. All the words looked like <u>tiny</u> ants on the page. He closed the book angrily. "I will never learn!" he cried.

6 "Sure you will," Dad said.

7 Every day at school, Jackson worked at his reading. His teacher helped him sound out the words. He tried to read many different books. Some of them were hard. Others were easy. All the work paid off. One day, Jackson picked up a new book. He read it without stopping.

8 "Very good!" said his teacher.

9 Jackson couldn't wait to show his parents that he could read. That night he read a new book for them. He knew all the words. When he was finished, Mom and Dad were very happy.

10 "Great job, Jackson!" they said. "You are a reader now."

GO ON.

Name _____   Date _____

PART 2: READING SELECTION #2

DIRECTIONS: For each question, circle the BEST answer. You may look back at the selection as often as necessary.

6 In paragraph 5, what does *tiny* mean?

A. moving

B. black

C. small

D. busy

7 Which of these BEST describes Jackson's mom and dad?

A. sad

B. helpful

C. angry

D. tired

8 Jackson did all of these in the story EXCEPT

A. read every day.

B. sound out words.

C. study spelling.

D. read easy books.

GO ON.

Name _____   Date _____

9 Why are Jackson's parents happy at the end of the story?

A. Jackson read them a new book.

B. Jackson learned his numbers.

C. Jackson went to school.

D. Jackson learned a new word.

10 What did Jackson learn about reading?

A. It is more fun than sports.

B. It teaches funny lessons.

C. It is easy for grown-ups.

D. It takes a lot of practice.

GO ON.

Name _____   Date _____

PART 2: CROSS-TEXT QUESTIONS

DIRECTIONS: Questions 11–12 ask about BOTH of the selections you read. For each question, circle the BEST answer. You may look back at the two selections as often as necessary.

11 What would be a good title for both of these selections?

A. *A Great Meal*

B. *Getting Discouraged*

C. *You Can Do It*

D. *My Brother Ben*

12 What is one way that these selections are alike?

A. Both are about learning to read.

B. Both are about chapter books.

C. Both are about a teacher.

D. Both are about Saturday.

STOP.

PART 2: WRITING IN RESPONSE TO READING
Tips for Using a Two-Column Chart

A two-column chart is a type of graphic organizer. You can use it to plan your writing. A two-column chart can help you figure out what you already know about your subject. It can also help you figure out what you need to know. This type of chart is helpful when you are showing how two things are alike or different.

Below is an example of a two-column chart. It compares an elephant and a house cat. The title of the chart is *Animal Differences*. The chart's title tells the main idea, or the topic. Each animal being compared has one column in which to put details. If some of your information does not fit the topic, you cannot put it in the chart. For example, in the chart below information about a robin would not fit the topic.

ANIMAL DIFFERENCES

Elephant	House Cat
large	small
eats plants	eats meat
has hair	has fur

GO ON.

PART 2: WRITING IN RESPONSE TO READING

Think about the people and their activities in the selections you just read. Then answer the following question.

Do you think that some of the activities that took place in both selections are ways of sharing stories?

Think about the first selection. Use the left column of the chart below to list what the people in "Special Saturday" did. Then think about the second selection. List what the people in "Jackson Reads" did. Using your notes from the chart, decide whether your answer to the question is YES or NO. Then explain your answer by using specific examples and details from "Special Saturday" and "Jackson Reads."

ACTIVITIES THAT TOOK PLACE IN THE SELECTIONS

Special Saturday	Jackson Reads
The family chooses a book to read.	Jackson tries to read to his mom and dad.

GO ON.

Name _____   Date _____

DRAFT

Remember to refer to the Revising and Editing Checklist on page 6 in this workbook as you develop your draft.

_____

_____

_____

_____

_____

_____

_____

_____

_____

_____

_____

GO ON.

Name _____ Date _____

FINAL COPY

Use the English/Language Arts Rubric chart on pages 4 and 5 in this workbook to check your writing and make changes.

_____

_____

_____

_____

_____

_____

_____

_____

_____

_____

_____

_____

_____

_____

STOP.

PART 1: WRITING FROM KNOWLEDGE AND EXPERIENCE

This test is divided into two parts that are all linked to one theme or important idea. The theme for this unit is **Sharing Stories.** Keep the theme in mind as you are taking this test.

In Part 1, you will be presented with a number of ways to write about the theme. You must choose ONLY ONE way. Begin Part 1 by reading the information provided. After you have finished reading, turn the page and begin writing a DRAFT. When you have completed your draft, use the REVISING AND EDITING CHECKLIST on page 6 in this workbook to review your writing. Then enter your final copy on the page marked FINAL COPY. You may use a dictionary, thesaurus, grammar book, or spelling book for Part 1 writing.

WRITE ABOUT THE THEME: Sharing Stories

Not all stories are make-believe. Some stories are true. You share and hear stories every day. When you tell a family member about something you did, you are sharing a story. When friends or family members tell you about something that happened, they are sharing a story with you. These true stories are part of our daily lives. We share them because they help us stay connected to people who are important to us.

Consider the following ideas for your piece of writing:
- Write about the differences between a true story and a make-believe story.
- Describe a favorite true story about one of your friends.
- Tell about a time when you shared a true story about yourself with someone.

You do not have to use the suggestions shown above. You can use your own idea about sharing stories for your piece of writing. As you write about **Sharing Stories,** use examples from real life, from what you read or watch, or from your imagination.

GO ON.

Use a separate sheet of paper for listing ideas, organizing your thoughts, or writing a rough draft. You may use the REVISING AND EDITING CHECKLIST on page 6 in this workbook to help you as you work on your draft.

When you are ready, you may begin your draft.

After you have finished your draft, you may use the English/Language Arts Rubric chart on pages 4 and 5 in this workbook to help you as you write your final copy.

GO ON.

Name _____   Date _____

FINAL COPY

Use the English/Language Arts Rubric chart on pages 4 and 5 in this workbook to check your writing and make changes.

_____

_____

_____

_____

_____

_____

_____

_____

_____

_____

_____

STOP.

PART 2: READING

DIRECTIONS

Read Selection 1. Answer the five multiple-choice questions that follow Selection 1. You may look back at the selection at any time.

Go on to Selection 2. Answer the five multiple-choice questions that follow Selection 2. You may look back at the selection at any time.

Then answer the two multiple-choice questions in the section called PART 2: CROSS-TEXT QUESTIONS.

As you answer the multiple-choice questions, choose the BEST answer. Do not worry if there are questions you cannot answer. Take your time and do as well as you can.

When you have finished reading the selections and answering all of the questions, you may wish to go back and check your work. Do not go on to the next section until you are told to do so.

GO ON.

Library Surprise

1 Every Tuesday Keesha's class went to the school library. Keesha didn't like the library. She never found any books she wanted to read.

2 Keesha sat in the library while her friends looked at books. The librarian saw her. "Why aren't you looking at books?" the librarian asked.

3 "I don't like anything here," Keesha said.

4 "I'm sure we can find something you will like," the librarian said. "Come with me."

5 Keesha followed the librarian. They went to a bookshelf filled with mysteries.

6 "How about these?" she asked.

7 "No," Keesha shook her head.

8 "Do you like animal stories?" asked the librarian. She pointed to other colorful books.

---

9 Keesha shook her head sadly.

10 The librarian showed Keesha books about science, history, and art. She took Keesha to the fiction <u>section</u>. They pulled out good storybooks. Keesha didn't want any of them.

11 Finally the librarian had an idea. She and Keesha went to another part of the library. A shelf was filled with sports books. Keesha was surprised.

12 "I didn't know there were so many sports books!" she said. She looked at the shelf. There were books about sports stars. She saw books about different sports like tennis, soccer, and baseball. Other books were filled with sports facts. Soon Keesha had picked two books to check out.

13 "I told you we would find something you would like," the librarian said with a smile.

GO ON.

MEAP Preparation and Practice **Level 2**

Name _____   Date _____

PART 2: READING SELECTION #1

DIRECTIONS: For each question, circle the BEST answer. You may look back at the selection as often as necessary.

1 Why doesn't Keesha like the library?

A. She does not know how to read.

B. She has read all the books.

C. She cannot find books she likes.

D. She cannot make up her mind.

2 Which word describes the librarian in this selection?

A. funny

B. proud

C. unhappy

D. helpful

3 The next time Keesha goes to the library, she will probably

A. look at more sports books.

B. sit by herself.

C. play a game.

D. read a science book.

GO ON.

Name _____   Date _____

4 The reader can tell that Keesha probably enjoys

A. taking care of pets.

B. doing experiments.

C. playing sports.

D. painting pictures.

5 In paragraph 10, what does the word *section* mean?

A. room

B. part of the library

C. chapter in a book

D. class

GO ON.

Making a Book

1 It takes many people to make a book. First, the writer creates an exciting story. The writer types the story into a computer and sends it to a publisher. The publisher reads the story. Together they have lots of new ideas about the story. The writer keeps writing new parts to the story until everyone is happy. But this is still just the beginning!

2 Next, an artist reads the story and begins to draw pictures. The artist uses bright colors to make the pictures come to life. When the pictures are done, the publisher uses a computer to put the words and the pictures together. But there is no book yet. Everything is still on a computer disk.

First, the writer creates an exciting story.

3 The disk then goes to a printer. At the printer, special computers read the disk. Giant presses copy each page of the book thousands of times onto huge rolls of paper. Special machines cut and trim all the pages to exactly the same size. Other machines make the book covers. One machine puts the pages inside the book <u>cover</u>. Another machine drops the books into boxes. Soon the brand-new book will be on bookshelves around the country.

Next, an artist reads the story and begins to draw pictures.

GO ON.

MEAP Preparation and Practice **Level 2**

Name _____   Date _____

PART 2: READING SELECTION #2

DIRECTIONS: For each question, circle the BEST answer. You may look back at the selection as often as necessary.

6 To make sure the story will make a good book, the writer meets with

A. an artist.

B. a publisher.

C. a computer.

D. a bookshop.

7 The reader can tell from the story that making a book

A. is easy.

B. takes two people.

C. is fast.

D. takes time.

8 Who works on a book last?

A. the publisher

B. the printer

C. the writer

D. the artist

GO ON.

Name _____   Date _____

9 In paragraph 3, what does the word *cover* mean?

A. a warm blanket

B. winter clothes

C. a roof on a house

D. something that is put over something else

10 Look at the diagram about a writer and an artist.

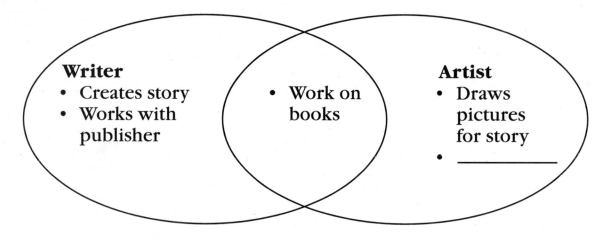

Which of these goes in the blank?

A. Trims pages

B. Sends disk to printer

C. Uses bright colors

D. Makes book covers

GO ON.

Name Chloe pennis   Date _____

PART 2: CROSS-TEXT QUESTIONS

DIRECTIONS: Questions 11–12 ask about BOTH of the selections you read. For each question, circle the BEST answer. You may look back at the two selections as often as necessary.

11 What is one difference between these selections?

A. One is a story and the other is an article.

B. One is a poem and the other is a story.

C. One is a story and the other is a biography.

D. One is an article and the other is a play.

12 What is one way that these selections are alike?

A. Both are about libraries.

B. Both are about books.

C. Both are about artists.

D. Both are about story time.

STOP.

PART 2: WRITING IN RESPONSE TO READING

Think about the people and their activities in the selections you just read. Then answer the following question.

Did most of the people in these selections contribute to sharing stories in some way?

Think about the people in each selection. You may wish to use a graphic organizer to keep track of the information that you find about the people in the selections. Using your notes, decide whether your answer to the question above is YES or NO. Then explain your answer by using specific examples and details from "Library Surprise" and "Making a Book." Be sure to show how the selections are alike.

GO ON.

Name _____   Date _____

FINAL COPY

Use the English/Language Arts Rubric chart on pages 4 and 5 in this workbook to check your writing and make changes.

_____

_____

_____

_____

_____

_____

_____

_____

_____

_____

_____

_____

STOP.

PART 1: WRITING FROM KNOWLEDGE AND EXPERIENCE

This test is divided into two parts that are all linked to one theme or important idea. The theme for this unit is **Kindness.** Refer to the Theme Connections pages at the end of each selection in Unit 2 in your Student Anthology for additional information about the theme. Keep the theme in mind as you are taking this test.

In Part 1, you will be presented with a number of ways to write about the theme. You must choose ONLY ONE way. After you have finished reading the information provided, begin writing a draft. When you have completed your draft, use the REVISING AND EDITING CHECKLIST on page 6 in this workbook to review your writing. Then enter your final copy on the page marked FINAL COPY. You may use a dictionary, thesaurus, grammar book, or spelling book for Part 1 writing.

Tips for Traits of Good Writing
Organizing Your Writing

For more information on the traits of good writing, turn to page 12 in the *Open Court Reading Language Arts Handbook.*

Good writing keeps your readers interested. They are comfortable with what they are reading. Your writing makes sense to them. How do you learn to write like that? You do it by making sure that your writing has organization. Writing that is organized has an interesting beginning. It has information or events that happen in a certain order. It also has an ending that satisfies your readers.

GO ON.

Look at the following passage. Look for its beginning, middle, and ending.

Ben was worried because he couldn't find his dog. Toby had been in the front yard that morning. Later when Ben went out to play with him, Toby was gone. The gate had come unlatched. That's how Toby got out.

Ben and his dad started looking around their neighborhood. First they checked the playground. Next they looked all through the park. Then they stopped at the lake where Dad took Ben and Toby so they could play "fetch." Toby just wasn't anywhere. Ben and Dad went back home. Ben felt discouraged and sad.

Late in the afternoon, the phone rang. Dad answered the phone. As he talked a big smile came over his face. "We'll be right there," he said and hung up the phone. "That was Mr. Jensen over on Maple Street. Toby just wandered into his back yard. Mr. Jensen found our phone number on Toby's collar." Ben was so happy that he felt like jumping up and down. He could hardly sit still in the car as they drove over to Maple Street to bring Toby home.

- Notice the first sentence of the passage. It is an interesting beginning. It tells about a problem that most readers will probably care about.

- Now look at the rest of the first paragraph and the second paragraph. These sentences tell what happened in an order that is easy to follow. The order of the events in the passage makes sense.

- Finally, look at the last paragraph. This ending is a good one because it tells readers what happened to Toby. Readers are glad that Toby is safe. How would you feel about this passage if it ended with the second paragraph? Passages without endings are not much fun to read.

Because this passage is well organized, it keeps the attention and interest of readers. Keep this information in mind as you write. Make sure that your writing has an interesting beginning. Keep the events in your writing in an order that makes sense. Close your story with an ending that leaves your readers satisfied.

GO ON.

WRITE ABOUT THE THEME: Kindness

Think back over the last few days. Can you remember being kind to someone or something? Can you remember how it made you feel? Being kind to each other and all living things is very healthy behavior. It is good for our minds and our bodies. It helps us lead happy lives. In addition to being good for us, being kind has a wonderful effect upon others. It helps them show kindness. Sometimes kind actions are returned in unexpected ways.

Consider the following ideas for your piece of writing:

- Write about a time when you showed kindness to a person or another living thing.

- Describe an act of kindness that you saw or heard about.

- Tell about a time when you were kind and someone returned your kindness.

You do not have to use the suggestions shown above. You can use your own idea about **Kindness** for your piece of writing. As you write about the theme, use examples from real life, from what you read or watch, or from your imagination.

Use a separate sheet of paper for listing ideas, organizing your thoughts, or writing a rough draft. You may use the REVISING AND EDITING CHECKLIST on page 6 in this workbook to help you as you work on your draft.

When you are ready, you may begin your draft.

After you have finished your draft, you may use the English/Language Arts Rubric chart on pages 4 and 5 in this workbook to help you as you write your final copy.

GO ON.

Name _____   Date _____

FINAL COPY

Use the English/Language Arts Rubric chart on pages 4 and 5 in this
workbook to check your writing and make changes.

_____

_____

_____

_____

_____

_____

_____

_____

_____

_____

_____

_____

STOP.

PART 2: READING

Tips for Reading Test Items Carefully

Reading carefully is a very important part of a multiple-choice test. If you don't read the questions and answers carefully, you will probably make a mistake. Read the paragraph below.

> Some animals can run faster than humans. Humans can run at a maximum speed of about 28 miles per hour. Cheetahs can run more than twice that fast. Their maximum speed is 70 miles per hour. A grizzly bear and a domestic cat can run just a little faster than a human. They can both run 30 miles per hour. A white-tailed deer also can run 30 miles per hour. Neither humans nor animals can run at these speeds for very long.

Notice that the paragraph above is comparing the running speeds of different animals to the running speed of humans. There are several facts in the paragraph that you must keep straight. Now read the question below word by word. Try not to skip over any words. Take special notice of any words in heavy or bold type.

1. Which of these is **not** mentioned in the paragraph?
    A. a domestic cat
    B. a mule deer
    C. a grizzly bear
    D. a cheetah

To find the correct answer, read every word in each answer choice carefully. Compare the answer choices to the same words in the paragraph.

- Answers A, C, and D are in the paragraph so they cannot be the right answer.

- Only B is **not** mentioned in the paragraph. White-tailed deer are mentioned in the seventh sentence, but mule deer are not. Just one word in answer B made it different from what was in the paragraph. Always be sure to read each word in an answer choice.

GO ON.

DIRECTIONS

Read Selection 1. Answer the five multiple-choice questions that follow Selection 1. You may look back at the selection at any time.

Go on to Selection 2. Answer the five multiple-choice questions that follow Selection 2. You may look back at the selection at any time.

Then answer the two multiple-choice questions in the section called PART 2: CROSS-TEXT QUESTIONS.

As you answer the multiple-choice questions, choose the BEST answer. Do not worry if there are questions you cannot answer. Take your time and do as well as you can.

When you have finished reading the selections and answering all of the questions, you may wish to go back and check your work. Do not go on to the next section until you are told to do so.

GO ON.

New Friends

1   Squirrel was in the forest. He was gathering acorns. He wanted to be ready for the coming winter. Suddenly the sky turned dark. Raindrops fell on the leaves. Squirrel tried to climb to his nest, but the rain got into his ears. The wind stung his eyes. Then he heard a voice say, "Come in here, quick!"

2   It was an animal Squirrel had never seen. She helped Squirrel into her burrow. It was warm and dry in the burrow. Squirrel said, "Thank you. I am Squirrel."

3   "Hello, I am Rabbit," she said. "I just moved here last week."

4   Rabbit gave Squirrel a towel to dry his fur. Then she put milk, sandwiches, and cookies on a small table. Squirrel and Rabbit ate lunch and talked. The storm blew outside. Soon they were very good friends.

5   Finally, the storm stopped. Squirrel wiped his mouth and said, "Thank you, Rabbit, for your kindness. There is an empty nest next door to me high up in the oak tree. Would you like to be my next-door neighbor?"

6   Rabbit said, "Thank you for the offer, Squirrel. I'm not very good at climbing trees. A nest high in the branches is not for me. But I would like to visit with you again. How about lunch next week?"

7   Squirrel agreed. He was happy to find a new friend.

GO ON.

Name _____   Date _____

PART 2: READING SELECTION #1

DIRECTIONS: For each question, circle the BEST answer. You may look back at the selection as often as necessary.

1 Squirrel meets Rabbit when he is

A. lost in the forest.

B. climbing a tree.

C. caught in a storm.

D. building a nest.

2 This story probably takes place in the

A. spring.

B. summer.

C. fall.

D. winter.

3 You can tell this story is make-believe because

A. Rabbit lives in a cozy burrow.

B. there are no people.

C. Squirrel and Rabbit live in the same forest.

D. the animals talk like people.

GO ON.

Name _____   Date _____

4 Look at this chart that shows causes and effects from the story.

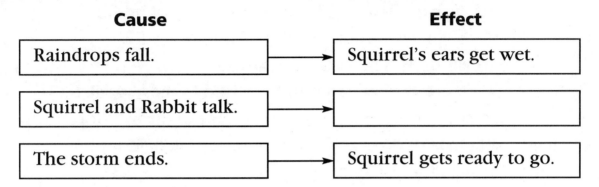

Cause	Effect
Raindrops fall. →	Squirrel's ears get wet.
Squirrel and Rabbit talk. →	
The storm ends. →	Squirrel gets ready to go.

Which of these belongs in the blank?

A. Rabbit decides to move.

B. They become good friends.

C. Squirrel dries his fur.

D. They eat lunch.

5 Rabbit gave Squirrel a towel because she wanted Squirrel to

A. feel comfortable.

B. stay for lunch.

C. climb up to his nest.

D. give her some acorns.

GO ON.

New Homes

1 Greyhounds are beautiful, fast dogs. Many people race these dogs. Greyhounds race for only a few years. After that, homes must be found for them. Special groups work to find homes for greyhounds who can't race anymore.

2 A group that helps animals find homes is called an adoption group. There are adoption groups for all kinds of dogs and cats. There are even adoption groups for horses and circus animals.

3 The people who help in these groups love greyhounds. They want every dog to find a good home. They work to make sure the dogs will be loved and cared for. Sometimes this is <u>hard</u>. Most greyhounds grow up on a racetrack.

Many of them are not used to living in a house with a family. Some groups teach the greyhounds to get ready for their new lives.

4   Most adoption groups ask people to fill out forms. The people write down what they are looking for in a pet. Sometimes they want a dog that likes children. Others need a dog that will get along with cats and other pets. The groups read the forms and try to find the perfect dog for each family.

5   The adoption groups tell the families about their new greyhound. Their new dog might like to sleep on soft pillows. It might even try to sleep on couches and beds. The dog also might be scared at first. It will need time to get used to its new home. After that, the greyhound will make a great family pet.

GO ON.

Name _____ Date _____

PART 2: READING SELECTION #2

DIRECTIONS: For each question, circle the BEST answer. You may look back at the selection as often as necessary.

6 The reader can tell that the author thinks greyhounds are

A. better than cats.

B. expensive.

C. nice dogs.

D. dangerous pets.

7 A greyhound would most likely sleep on a

A. wooden chair.

B. kitchen floor.

C. folded blanket.

D. warm driveway.

8 This story was written mainly to

A. show how fast greyhounds are.

B. tell how to pick a family pet.

C. describe why greyhounds get scared.

D. tell how greyhounds find new homes.

GO ON.

Name _____   Date _____

9 In paragraph 3, what does the word *hard* mean?

A. sad

B. not easy

C. stiff

D. not fun

10 What does the selection say might happen at first to a greyhound in a new home?

A. It might run and get lost.

B. It might want to stay inside its cage.

C. It might be a little scared.

D. It might be sad.

GO ON.

Name _____   Date _____

PART 2: CROSS-TEXT QUESTIONS

DIRECTIONS: Questions 11–12 ask about BOTH of the selections you read. For each question, circle the BEST answer. You may look back at the two selections as often as necessary.

11 What would be a good title for both these selections?

A. Good Food

B. The Kindness of Strangers

C. Run for Your Life

D. A Sudden Storm

12 These selections are mostly about

A. racing.

B. adoption.

C. animals.

D. life in the forest.

STOP.

PART 2: WRITING IN RESPONSE TO READING

Tips for Using a Venn Diagram

A Venn diagram is a type of graphic organizer used to show how two things are alike and different. A Venn diagram has a place to write how the two things are different. There is also a place to write how the two things are alike.

Below is an example of a Venn diagram. The information in the left side of the diagram tells ways that baseball is different from basketball. The information in the right side of the diagram tells ways that basketball is different from baseball. The information in the middle tells how the two sports are alike.

Use a Venn diagram to help you gather and organize information. Then use the information when you do the first draft of your writing.

Baseball
- 9-member team
- usually played outside
- game has 9 untimed innings

- uses a ball
- team sport

Basketball
- 5-member team
- usually played inside
- game has 4 timed quarters

GO ON.

PART 2: WRITING IN RESPONSE TO READING

DIRECTIONS: Think about what happened in the selections you just read. Then answer the following question.

Do you think the ways that kindness was shown in these selections were mostly alike or mostly different?

Think about the first selection. Use the left side of the Venn diagram below to list ways that the kindness shown in "New Friends" was different from the kindness shown in "New Homes." Then think about the second selection. Use the right side of the Venn diagram to list ways that kindness shown in "New Homes" was different from the kindness shown in "New Friends." In the center of the Venn diagram, list the ways that the kindness shown in both selections was alike. Using the notes from the Venn diagram, decide whether your answer to the question is MOSTLY ALIKE or MOSTLY DIFFERENT. Then explain your answer by using specific examples and details from "New Friends" and "New Homes."

New Friends
- Rabbit gave squirrel a towel

- Animals being shown kindness in a new home

New Homes
- Adoption groups help find greyhounds homes

GO ON.

Name _____   Date _____

DRAFT

Remember to refer to the Revising and Editing Checklist on page 6 in this workbook as you develop your draft.

_____

_____

_____

_____

_____

_____

_____

_____

_____

_____

_____

GO ON.

Name _____ Date _____

FINAL COPY

Use the English/Language Arts Rubric chart on pages 4 and 5 in this
workbook to check your writing and make changes.

_____

_____

_____

_____

_____

_____

_____

_____

_____

_____

_____

STOP.

PART 1: WRITING FROM KNOWLEDGE AND EXPERIENCE

This test is divided into two parts that are all linked to one theme or important idea. The theme for this unit is **Kindness.** Keep the theme in mind as you are taking this test.

In Part 1, you will be presented with a number of ways to write about the theme. You must choose ONLY ONE way. After you have finished reading the information provided, begin writing a draft. When you have completed your draft, use the REVISING AND EDITING CHECKLIST on page 6 in this workbook to review your writing. Then enter your final copy on the page marked FINAL COPY. You may use a dictionary, thesaurus, grammar book, or spelling book for Part 1 writing.

GO ON.

WRITE ABOUT THE THEME: Kindness

Being kind isn't always easy. It can mean going out of your way to help someone. It can mean keeping your temper when you want to be impatient or angry. It can also mean giving up something you really like or really want to do. Sometimes being kind isn't the easiest thing, but most of the time you can tell that it is the right thing. Helping others, sharing what you have, and treating others with respect are ways to show kindness.

Consider the following ideas for your piece of writing:
- Write about a time when you or someone you know showed kindness by sharing.
- Describe an act of kindness in which you or someone you know gave up something to be kind.
- Tell about a time when it was hard to be kind.

You do not have to use the suggestions shown above. You can use your own idea about **Kindness** for your piece of writing. As you write about the theme, use examples from real life, from what you read or watch, or from your imagination.

Use a separate sheet of paper for listing ideas, organizing your thoughts, or writing a rough draft. You may use the REVISING AND EDITING CHECKLIST on page 6 in this workbook to help you as you work on your draft.

When you are ready, you may begin your draft.

After you have finished your draft, you may use the English/Language Arts Rubric chart on pages 4 and 5 in this workbook to help you as you write your final copy.

GO ON.

Name _____ Date _____

FINAL COPY

Use the English/Language Arts Rubric chart on pages 4 and 5 in this
workbook to check your writing and make changes.

_____

_____

_____

_____

_____

_____

_____

_____

_____

_____

_____

STOP.

PART 2: READING

DIRECTIONS

Read Selection 1. Answer the five multiple-choice questions that follow Selection 1. You may look back at the selection at any time.

Go on to Selection 2. Answer the five multiple-choice questions that follow Selection 2. You may look back at the selection at any time.

Then answer the two multiple-choice questions in the section called PART 2: CROSS-TEXT QUESTIONS.

As you answer the multiple-choice questions, choose the BEST answer. Do not worry if there are questions you cannot answer. Take your time and do as well as you can.

When you have finished reading the selections and answering all of the questions, you may wish to go back and check your work. Do not go on to the next section until you are told to do so.

GO ON.

Saying Thanks

1   It was raining in the city. Jaheer drove his taxi along the wet city streets. He looked out his window and saw a tiny, black puppy. Jaheer felt sorry for the puppy. He took the puppy home. He dried her off and fed her.

2   "I'll bet someone is looking for this puppy," Jaheer thought. He asked people on the street if they were looking for a puppy. Everyone said no. Then Jaheer saw a sign on a lamppost. It had a phone number and a picture of the puppy. Jaheer went home and called the number.

3   A man answered the phone. "I found your puppy," Jaheer said to the man. Soon, the man knocked on Jaheer's door. A little girl was with the man.

4 "Buffy!" the girl cried when she saw the puppy. Buffy barked and ran into the little girl's arms.

5 "Thank you, sir," said the man. He shook Jaheer's hand. Jaheer's eyes opened wide. The man was Johnathan King, the famous basketball star!

6 "You were very kind," Mr. King said. "I would like to show my thanks. Here are some tickets to the game Sunday." He handed Jaheer four tickets.

7 "Thank you," Jaheer said. "I'm glad I could help."

8 "See you Sunday," the little girl said. Buffy wagged her tail and barked.

GO ON.

Name _____   Date _____

PART 2: READING SELECTION #1

DIRECTIONS: For each question, circle the BEST answer. You may look back at the selection as often as necessary.

1 How did Jaheer find the puppy's owner?

A. He read the newspaper.

B. He talked to neighbors.

C. He studied the dog's tags.

D. He saw a sign on a lamppost.

2 How does the little girl change in the story?

A. from lost to found

B. from sad to happy

C. from worried to sad

D. from pleased to worried

3 The title "Saying Thanks" is connected to which part of the story?

A. Jaheer taking the puppy home

B. Jaheer calling the puppy's owner

C. the puppy running to the little girl

D. Mr. King giving Jaheer tickets

GO ON.

Name _____   Date _____

4 What did Mr. King do RIGHT AFTER he thanked Jaheer?

A. He called the phone number.

B. He gave Buffy a bath.

C. He shook Jaheer's hand.

D. He gave Jaheer the tickets.

5 Look at this web about Jaheer.

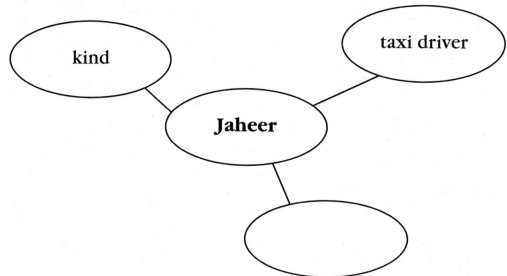

Which of these belongs in the empty circle?

A. likes dogs

B. father

C. coaches basketball

D. ticket seller

GO ON.

Bird Land

1   Tyrell's Uncle Leon had the strangest yard in the neighborhood. It was filled with bird feeders. There were big bird feeders, small bird feeders, long bird feeders, and short bird feeders. Some feeders hung from tree branches. Others sat on top of poles. One corner of the yard was filled with old rotting logs. Uncle Leon even had built a large water garden in the middle of the yard.

2   "Why do you have so many bird feeders?" Tyrell asked his uncle one day. "And why don't you move the old logs out of your yard?"

3   Uncle Leon smiled. "When the seasons change, different birds come to this area," he said. "Some are flying south for winter. Others live here year-round. Some live here only in the summer. All of these birds like different foods.

4   "Some like sunflower seeds. Others like <u>plain</u> birdseed. I put different seeds in each feeder to attract all kinds of birds.

5   "Some birds eat insects that live in rotting trees," he explained. "Others like bugs that live around water. All birds need a little water. That's why I have the logs and the water garden in the yard."

6   "It is a bird land at Uncle Leon's house," Tyrell said with a laugh.

GO ON.

Name _____   Date _____

PART 2: READING SELECTION #2

DIRECTIONS: For each question, circle the BEST answer. You may look back at the selection as often as necessary.

6 In paragraph 4, what does the word *plain* mean?

A. mixed

B. simple

C. fancy

D. wet

7 Where did Uncle Leon put the rotting logs?

A. around the water garden

B. under the trees

C. in the corner of the yard

D. in the center of the yard

8 Every bird in Uncle Leon's yard

A. needs a little water.

B. flies south in the winter.

C. stays only in the summer.

D. eats sunflower seeds.

GO ON.

Name _____ Date _____

9 Uncle Leon has all of these bird feeders EXCEPT

A. hanging.

B. small.

C. floating.

D. long.

10 You can tell that Uncle Leon wants

A. Tyrell to fill the feeders.

B. to build a bigger pond.

C. a few more bird feeders.

D. all birds to feel welcome.

GO ON.

PART 2: CROSS-TEXT QUESTIONS

DIRECTIONS: Questions 11–12 ask about BOTH of the selections you read. For each question, circle the BEST answer. You may look back at the two selections as often as necessary.

11 What is one way in which these selections are alike?

A. They are both biographies.

B. They are both articles.

C. They are both stories.

D. They are both poems.

12 Both selections have people and _____ in them.

A. taxi cabs

B. bird feeders

C. rotting logs

D. animals

STOP.

PART 2: WRITING IN RESPONSE TO READING

DIRECTIONS: Think about the people and their activities in the selections you just read. Then answer the following question.

Do you think that any of the people in these selections went out of their way or gave up something to be kind?

Think about both selections. Decide whether your answer to the question is YES or NO. You may wish to use a graphic organizer to keep track of information from each selection. Then explain your answer by using specific examples and details from "Saying Thanks" and "Bird Land."

GO ON.

Name _____   Date _____

FINAL COPY

Use the English/Language Arts Rubric chart on pages 4 and 5 in this workbook to check your writing and make changes.

_____

_____

_____

_____

_____

_____

_____

_____

_____

_____

_____

_____

STOP.

PART 1: WRITING FROM KNOWLEDGE AND EXPERIENCE

This test is divided into two parts that are all linked to one theme or important idea. The theme for this unit is **Look Again.** Refer to the Theme Connections pages at the end of each selection in Unit 3 in your Student Anthology for additional information about the theme. Keep the theme in mind as you are taking this test.

In Part 1, you will be presented with a number of ways to write about the theme. You must choose ONLY ONE way. After you have finished reading the information provided, begin writing a draft. When you have completed your draft, use the REVISING AND EDITING CHECKLIST on page 6 in this workbook to review your writing. Then enter your final copy on the page marked FINAL COPY. You may use a dictionary, thesaurus, grammar book, or spelling book for Part 1 writing.

Tips for Traits of Good Writing
Developing Voice in Your Writing

For more information on the traits of good writing, turn to page 12 in the *Open Court Reading Language Arts Handbook.*

A writer's voice is the way he or she connects with readers. Voice grabs the readers' attention. Voice gives personality to your writing. It is the writer's special way of sharing ideas and feelings. When you write, your voice can show that you really care about your subject and your readers.

GO ON.

Read the passage below. As you read, notice the writer's voice. It will tell you what the writer is like.

> My pet snake's name is Roger. Roger and I have been friends for two years. A snake is a great pet. You don't have to take it for walks. You don't have to give it a bath. Snakes are very clean animals.
>
> You would think that my family would be happy that I have such a care-free pet. They're not. It makes them nervous when Roger gets out of his cage. They don't like how he just appears in a chair or on a bed. I tell them that Roger just got bored. He wanted a change of scenery. Everybody needs a little change, now and then.

The very first sentence of the passage probably grabbed your attention. As you read the rest of the story, maybe you began to think that the writer has a good sense of humor. You also probably got the feeling that he or she is interested in the subject. The writer's interest in the subject and in connecting with the readers gives the writing its own special voice.

Now, read the paragraph below.

> My snake's name is Roger. A snake is a good pet. My family doesn't like Roger. They don't like it when he gets out of his cage. They want him to stay in it.

Notice how there is no clear voice in the writing. This writer doesn't seem to have much enthusiasm for the topic. Your writing will be interesting, fun to read, and easy to remember if it has voice.

GO ON.

WRITE ABOUT THE THEME: Look Again

Sometimes we miss seeing something when we're looking right at it. In nature, not being seen is important for animals. The color of their skin, scales, or fur is the same as their surroundings. Some animals use their coloring to catch other animals. They can get up close before they are noticed. Other animals use their coloring as protection. It keeps them hidden from animals who would like to catch them. The next time you are in the woods or in a park, look for an animal that is "hiding in plain sight."

Consider the following ideas for your piece of writing:

- Write about a time when you or someone you know saw an animal with protective coloring.

- Describe an animal that has coloring similar to its surroundings and how the animal uses its coloring.

- Tell about a time when you or someone you know overlooked something because you were not paying attention.

You do not have to use the suggestions shown above. You can use your own idea about **Look Again** for your piece of writing. As you write about the theme, use examples from real life, from what you read or watch, or from your imagination.

Use a separate sheet of paper for listing ideas, organizing your thoughts, or writing a rough draft. You may use the REVISING AND EDITING CHECKLIST on page 6 in this workbook to help you as you work on your draft.

When you are ready, you may begin your draft.

After you have finished your draft, you may use the English/Language Arts Rubric chart on pages 4 and 5 in this workbook to help you as you write your final copy.

GO ON.

Name _____ Date _____

FINAL COPY

Use the English/Language Arts Rubric chart on pages 4 and 5 in this workbook to check your writing and make changes.

_____

_____

_____

_____

_____

_____

_____

_____

_____

_____

_____

_____

STOP.

PART 2: READING

Tips for Finding the Main Idea

On a multiple-choice test, you might be asked the main idea of a selection. The main idea is what a selection is mostly about. You find the main idea by thinking about the whole story or article.

Read the paragraph below. Think about what the main idea might be.

> Rachel and her mother got to the park early on Saturday morning. They brought bread to feed the ducks. The ducks really liked their bread breakfast. Rachel and her mother walked around the lake. They watched people flying colored kites. The kites were beautiful against the bright blue sky. They watched people roller skating along the paths. At noon Rachel and her mother ate their picnic lunch. After lunch they listened to people playing songs on guitars and flutes. They left the park late in the afternoon. They had a wonderful day.

Now read this question.

1. What is this paragraph mostly about?
   A. feeding bread to the ducks
   B. eating a picnic lunch
   C. spending a day at the park
   D. seeing zoo animals

Notice that the question does not include the words "main idea." The main idea is what a story or article is mostly about. Whenever you see the words "mostly about" in a question, you are looking for the main idea. Look now at the answer choices.

- Feeding bread to the ducks is just one detail in the paragraph. It is not what the paragraph is mostly about. Answer A can't be right.

- Like Answer A, Answer B is just one detail of the paragraph.

- There is nothing in the paragraph about seeing zoo animals. So, Answer D is not right.

- Answer C is correct. It tells about the whole paragraph. The paragraph is mostly about spending a day at the park.

GO ON.

DIRECTIONS

Read Selection 1. Answer the five multiple-choice questions that follow Selection 1. You may look back at the selection at any time.

Go on to Selection 2. Answer the five multiple-choice questions that follow Selection 2. You may look back at the selection at any time.

Then answer the two multiple-choice questions in the section called PART 2: CROSS-TEXT QUESTIONS.

As you answer the multiple-choice questions, choose the BEST answer. Do not worry if there are questions you cannot answer. Take your time and do as well as you can.

When you have finished reading the selections and answering all of the questions, you may wish to go back and check your work. Do not go on to the next section until you are told to do so.

GO ON.

A Funny Story

1   Derrick loved his dog, Socks. Derrick named him Socks because the dog had four white paws.

2   One day Derrick and Dad took Socks to the animal doctor. Derrick held Socks in his lap while they drove.

3   "Dad, why does Socks have white feet?" he asked.

4   "Well," Dad said, "Socks lived on a farm. He had many brothers and sisters. His mother had a hard time looking out for all her babies. Socks liked to get into trouble.

5   "One day Socks went exploring. He climbed out of the cozy box where he was born. He sniffed the hay. He made friends with the cows. Finally he came to a quiet corner of the barn. There were strange noises coming from the corner. He peeked in. A mother cat and her kittens were living in the corner.

MEAP Preparation and Practice **Level 2**

6 "The mother cat was afraid that Socks would hurt her babies. She growled at Socks. Socks was frightened. He ran through the barn, but he got lost. He ran right into a can of white paint! The paint spilled all over his feet. He did not bother to wipe it off. He just went back to his box. And that's how he got his white feet."

7 Derrick rubbed his dog's feet. It didn't look like paint. Socks licked his nose. Derrick grinned.

8 "That's a good story, Dad," Derrick said. "But I'm pretty sure it didn't happen that way."

9 Dad smiled. "Maybe not," he said. "But it is a good story, isn't it?"

GO ON.

Name _____   Date _____

PART 2: READING SELECTION #1

DIRECTIONS: For each question, circle the BEST answer. You may look back at the selection as often as necessary.

1 In paragraph 4, what does *looking out for* mean?

A. peeking at

B. taking care of

C. hunting for

D. finding

2 Dad's story is a make-believe story about

A. when Socks was born.

B. how Socks joined the family.

C. why Socks does not feel well.

D. how Socks got his white feet.

3 Which of these BEST describes Socks, according to Dad?

A. lonely

B. curious

C. sleepy

D. noisy

GO ON.

Name _____   Date _____

4 Which of these scared Socks in the story?

A. a cow

B. a person

C. a cat

D. a chicken

5 What did Socks do RIGHT BEFORE he met the mother cat?

A. He spilled some paint.

B. He saw some cows.

C. He sniffed some hay.

D. He found some food.

GO ON.

The Pheasant

1   Andrea loved afternoon walks with her grandfather. They usually went to the large field behind the barn. It was Andrea's favorite place to go.

2   This afternoon was bright and sunny. Andrea and Grandpa watched the tadpoles in the creek. They built a boat out of sticks and leaves. Andrea let it go in the water, and it floated away. Grandpa picked some flowers for Grandma. Andrea saw some flowers near a large pile of <u>brush</u>. She started to pick them. Suddenly, the bush rustled and shook! A brown bird burst out and flew away.

3   "What was that?" Andrea said.

4   "That was a pheasant, I believe," Grandpa said.

5 "I didn't even see it!" Andrea said. "And I was so close."

6 Grandpa smiled. "Pheasants are good at hiding," he said. "That was a female. Their dull brown feathers blend in with the brush. It makes it hard for predators to see them. Male pheasants have brighter colors. Even so, they are hard to see in weeds and brush."

7 "That's smart," Andrea asked.

8 Andrea peeked into the brush. She saw a nest with some eggs in it. "The pheasant must have been sitting on its nest," Andrea said.

9 Grandpa looked at the nest. "That pheasant will have a big family soon," he said. Then he smiled at Andrea. "We'll have to look for them on our next field walk."

GO ON.

Name _____   Date _____

PART 2: READING SELECTION #2

DIRECTIONS: For each question, circle the BEST answer. You may look back at the selection as often as necessary.

6 In paragraph 2, what does the word *brush* mean?

A. to wipe something off quickly

B. something you use for scrubbing

C. thick bushes and their branches

D. something you use on your hair

7 What surprised Andrea the MOST in this story?

A. the tadpoles

B. the boat

C. the flowers

D. the pheasant

8 BEFORE the bird flew away, what was it probably doing?

A. looking for food

B. sitting on eggs

C. making a nest

D. trying to sleep

GO ON.

Name _____   Date _____

9 Where does this story take place?

A. in a field

B. in a barn

C. in a garden

D. in a park

10 Look at the chart below. It shows the order of some events in the story.

Andrea and Grandpa took a walk in the field.
They picked some flowers for Grandma.
They saw a nest with eggs in it.

Which of these belongs in the empty box?

A. Tadpoles swim in the creek.

B. Andrea and Grandpa built a boat of sticks and twigs.

C. A brown bird burst out of a bush.

D. Andrea played in the creek.

GO ON.

Name _____ Date _____

PART 2: CROSS-TEXT QUESTIONS

DIRECTIONS: Questions 11–12 ask about BOTH of the selections you read. For each question, circle the BEST answer. You may look back at the two selections as often as necessary.

11 What is one way in which these selections are alike?

A. Both selections are articles.

B. Both selections are poems.

C. Both selections are plays.

D. Both selections are stories.

12 Which of the following statements is true?

A. The people in each selection go for a walk.

B. There are wild animals in both selections.

C. The people in each selection are relatives.

D. A person in each selection tells a story.

STOP.

PART 2: WRITING IN RESPONSE TO READING

Tips for Using a T-Chart

A T-Chart is a type of graphic organizer. You can use it to do some planning before you begin to write. It is a good tool when you want to show how two things are different. The T-Chart has a place for you to write how the two things are different.

Below is an example of a T-Chart. It shows some of the ways that two boys are different. The information in the left side of the chart tells ways that Paul is different from Richard. The information in the right side of the chart tells ways that Richard is different from Paul.

Use a T-Chart to help you gather and organize information. Then use the notes you make on the chart when you do the first draft of your writing.

Paul	Richard
Likes sports	Likes computers
Likes to be outdoors	Likes to be indoors
Favorite food is pizza	Favorite food is spaghetti
Favorite subject is science	Favorite subject is math

GO ON.

PART 2: WRITING IN RESPONSE TO READING

DIRECTIONS: Think about the animals in the selections that you just read. Then answer the following question.

Do you think that protective coloring is more important for wild animals than for pets?

Think about the first selection. Use the left side of the T-Chart below to list things that you know about Socks in "A Funny Story." Then think about the second selection. Use the right side of the T-Chart to list things that you know about the pheasant in "The Pheasant." Using the notes from the chart, decide whether your answer to the question above is YES or NO. Then explain your answer by using specific examples and details from "A Funny Story" and "The Pheasant."

Socks	Pheasant
Has four white paws	Is brown

GO ON.

Name _____   Date _____

DRAFT

Remember to refer to the Revising and Editing Checklist on page 6 in this workbook as you develop your draft.

_____

_____

_____

_____

_____

_____

_____

_____

_____

_____

_____

_____

GO ON.

Name _____ Date _____

FINAL COPY

Use the English/Language Arts Rubric chart on pages 4 and 5 in this workbook to check your writing and make changes.

_____

_____

_____

_____

_____

_____

_____

_____

_____

_____

_____

_____

_____

STOP.

PART 1: WRITING FROM KNOWLEDGE AND EXPERIENCE

This test is divided into two parts that are all linked to one theme or important idea. The theme for this unit is **Look Again.** Keep the theme in mind as you are taking this test.

In Part 1, you will be presented with a number of ways to write about the theme. You must choose ONLY ONE way. After you have finished reading the information provided, begin writing a draft. When you have completed your draft, use the REVISING AND EDITING CHECKLIST on page 6 in this workbook to review your writing. Then enter your final copy on the page marked FINAL COPY. You may use a dictionary, thesaurus, grammar book, or spelling book for Part 1 writing.

GO ON.

WRITE ABOUT THE THEME: Look Again

There is a type of puzzle called Hidden Pictures. The artist draws a picture and hides some items in the picture. The hidden items don't really belong in the picture, but they are there. Here is the interesting thing about Hidden Picture puzzles. Unless you look very carefully, you don't even notice the things that don't belong. You don't see them because you don't expect to see them. Sometimes our world is like a Hidden Puzzle. There are things waiting to be seen if we would just take the time to notice.

Consider the following ideas for your piece of writing:

- Write about a time when you or someone you know noticed something in a place where it was not expected.

- Describe a Hidden Puzzle that you might create and explain what items you would hide in it.

- Tell about a time when you or someone you know hid something in an unexpected place.

You do not have to use the suggestions shown above. You can use your own idea about **Look Again** for your piece of writing. As you write about the theme, use examples from real life, from what you read or watch, or from your imagination.

Use a separate sheet of paper for listing ideas, organizing your thoughts, or writing a rough draft. You may use the REVISING AND EDITING CHECKLIST on page 6 in this workbook to help you as you work on your draft.

When you are ready, you may begin your draft.

After you have finished your draft, you may use the English/Language Arts Rubric chart on pages 4 and 5 in this workbook to help you as you write your final copy.

GO ON.

Name _____   Date _____

FINAL COPY

Use the English/Language Arts Rubric chart on pages 4 and 5 in this workbook to check your writing and make changes.

_____

_____

_____

_____

_____

_____

_____

_____

_____

_____

_____

_____

STOP.

PART 2: READING

DIRECTIONS

Read Selection 1. Answer the five multiple-choice questions that follow Selection 1. You may look back at the selection at any time.

Go on to Selection 2. Answer the five multiple-choice questions that follow Selection 2. You may look back at the selection at any time.

Then answer the two multiple-choice questions in the section called PART 2: CROSS-TEXT QUESTIONS.

As you answer the multiple-choice questions, choose the BEST answer. Do not worry if there are questions you cannot answer. Take your time and do as well as you can.

When you have finished reading the selections and answering all of the questions, you may wish to go back and check your work. Do not go on to the next section until you are told to do so.

GO ON.

Learning to Hide

1 The forest was dim and cool. Spots of sunlight shone through the tall trees. Mother Deer and Fawn walked quietly through the woods.

2 Mother Deer stopped and sniffed the air. "Fawn," she said, "there is sweet grass in a meadow nearby. I must go see if it is safe. Stay here while I am gone."

3 "What if someone sees me?" Fawn asked.

4 "No one will see you," Mother Deer said. "Your brown fur and white spots look like the shadows in the forest. If you stand very still, no one can see you."

5 Mother Deer gently licked Fawn's cheek. Then she disappeared down the path. Fawn stood very still. No one saw him. Soon Mother Deer came back.

6 "The meadow is safe," she said. "Come with me."

7 Fawn followed Mother Deer to the meadow. They stayed near the shade of the tall trees at the edge of the forest. Fawn saw a large, square shape at the other end of the meadow.

8 "What's that?" he asked.

9 "That is where the humans live," Mother Deer said. "You don't have to be afraid of them. But don't go too close to them."

10 Mother Deer ate the sweet grass. Soon Fawn was ready for a nap. "Lie still in the tall grasses," Mother Deer said. "Nothing can see you then."

11 Fawn lay down and closed his eyes. It had been a busy morning.

GO ON.

Name _____ Date _____

PART 2: READING SELECTION #1

DIRECTIONS: For each question, circle the BEST answer. You may look back at the selection as often as necessary.

1 What do Fawn's brown fur and white spots look like?

A. sunlight

B. clouds

C. shadows

D. snow

2 Mother Deer licks Fawn's cheek because she

A. cares about him.

B. is afraid.

C. wants to clean him.

D. is worried.

3 Look at the cause-and-effect chart.

Cause

Fawn walks quietly.
Fawn sleeps in tall grasses.

Effect

Fawn stays safe.

Which sentence belongs in the blank box?

A. Fawn stands very still.

B. Fawn goes to the meadow.

C. Fawn eats grass.

D. Fawn gets tired.

GO ON.

Name _____   Date _____

4 The reader can tell that Fawn has never

A. slept in a meadow before.

B. seen a house before.

C. seen his mother before.

D. eaten sweet grass before.

5 What does Mother Deer teach Fawn?

A. how to eat sweet grass

B. how to look for humans

C. how to walk

D. how to hide in the forest

GO ON.

Hiding

1   Animals hide themselves in many ways. This is known as camouflage. Insects, birds, mammals, and fish use different kinds of camouflage. Animals use camouflage to protect themselves and their <u>young</u> and to help them hunt for food.

2   Some animals use their color to keep them safe. Snowshoe rabbits live in snowy areas. In the winter they have white fur. This makes them invisible in the snow. In the summer, their fur turns brown.

3   The female killdeer lays spotted eggs in areas with gravel. The eggs blend in with the small rocks. A bird called a bittern has stripes along its body. These stripes let it blend in with the water reeds and grasses where it lives.

4   A few animals can even change their color. The flounder, a kind of fish, can change color to match the ocean floor. Frogs, toads, and crabs may become darker or lighter to match the area around them.

5   Some animals look like plants. The praying mantis looks like a leafy twig. One kind of frog looks like a dead leaf. This helps the frog hide on the forest floor.

---

6 Some animals use camouflage to be better hunters. The lion's sandy color blends into the dry, brown African plains where it lives. A tiger's stripes help it hide in the jungle. Prey have a hard time seeing these hunters because of their coloring.

7 Camouflage is useful for wild animals. It keeps some animals safe. It also helps other animals catch the prey they need to live.

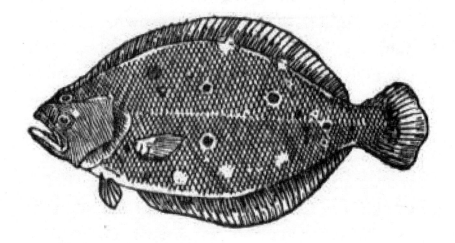

The flounder can change colors to match the bottom of the ocean where it lives.

GO ON.

Name _____   Date _____

PART 2: READING SELECTION #2

DIRECTIONS: For each question, circle the BEST answer. You may look back at the selection as often as necessary.

6 Camouflage is used for all of these except

A. hiding from danger.

B. protecting young.

C. running faster.

D. hunting for food.

7 If tigers didn't have stripes, they would probably

A. have a more difficult time catching food.

B. have to live in zoos.

C. start eating plants.

D. have spots instead.

8 You can tell from the story that

A. camouflage helps many animals survive.

B. camouflage is useless to prey.

C. animals change color to be noticed.

D. it is easier for animals to hide underwater.

GO ON.

Name _____ Date _____

9 In paragraph 1, what does the word *young* mean?

A. adults

B. babies

C. parents

D. friends

10 Camouflage helps animals

A. see their enemies.

B. eat their food.

C. make new friends.

D. look like where they live.

GO ON.

Name _____   Date _____

PART 2: CROSS-TEXT QUESTIONS

DIRECTIONS: Questions 11–12 ask about BOTH of the selections you read. For each question, circle the BEST answer. You may look back at the two selections as often as necessary.

11 What is one way in which these selections are different?

A. One is an article and the other is a story.

B. One is a biography and the other is an article.

C. One is a story and the other is a poem.

D. One is a play and the other is a poem.

12 Which of the following statements is true?

A. There are no animals in these selections.

B. Both selections take place in the winter.

C. Both selections describe how animals stay out of sight.

D. There are people in both of these selections.

STOP.

PART 2: WRITING IN RESPONSE TO READING

Think about the most important parts of the selections you just read. Then answer the following question.

Do you think that all animals hide themselves in the same way?

You may want to use a graphic organizer to collect information from both selections about how animals hide themselves. After you read over your notes, decide whether your answer to the question above is YES or NO. Explain your answer by using specific examples and details from "Learning to Hide" and "Hiding."

GO ON.

Name _____   Date _____

FINAL COPY

Use the English/Language Arts Rubric chart on pages 4 and 5 in this workbook to check your writing and make changes.

_____

_____

_____

_____

_____

_____

_____

_____

_____

_____

_____

_____

_____

STOP.

PART 1: WRITING FROM KNOWLEDGE AND EXPERIENCE

This test is divided into two parts that are all linked to one theme or important idea. The theme for this unit is **Fossils.** Refer to the Theme Connections pages at the end of each selection in Unit 4 in your Student Anthology for additional information about the theme. Keep the theme in mind as you are taking this test.

In Part 1, you will be presented with a number of ways to write about the theme. You must choose ONLY ONE way. After you have finished reading the information provided, begin writing a draft. When you have completed your draft, use the REVISING AND EDITING CHECKLIST on page 6 in this workbook to review your writing. Then enter your final copy on the page marked FINAL COPY. You may use a dictionary, thesaurus, grammar book, or spelling book for Part 1 writing.

Tips for Traits of Good Writing
Improving Word Choice in Writing

For more information on the traits of good writing, turn to page 13 in the *Open Court Reading Language Arts Handbook*.

The words you choose can help your writing come alive. They can also put your reader to sleep. Words can paint a picture in your reader's mind. Those are the kinds of words you want to use. They will help your reader see, hear, and feel your ideas. Think about a time when you were really excited about something you were reading. The writer made you feel as if you were right there. That writer chose words that put pictures, sounds, and feelings into your mind.

GO ON.

Read the paragraphs below. As you read, notice the writer's choice of words. What pictures, sounds, and feelings do you experience as you read?

> I will never forget my first circus. As we sat down on the hard, wooden seats, I looked around. Bright flags and streamers were floating from all the poles of the big tent. In the distance I could hear the elephants trumpeting and the big cats growling. Before long, they would be in the center ring performing their tricks.
>
> The clowns were already inside the tent. They ran along the rows of spectators. They clapped their hands and blew horns and whistles. The hot popcorn and roasted peanuts Dad and I had bought smelled wonderful. They tasted even better. Just then a tall man in a red jacket, white pants, and black boots stepped into the center ring. He welcomed us in a deep, booming voice. Then the music started and the circus began.

The writer of the paragraphs above chose words carefully. Could you see the flags and streamers? Could you hear the animals? Could you smell and taste the popcorn and peanuts? Could you see and hear the ringmaster? The writer helped you to use your imagination to experience the circus.

Now, read the paragraph below. It is on the same subject but without careful word choices.

> I will never forget my first circus. As we sat down, I looked around the tent. In the distance I could hear some animals. The clowns were already inside the tent. They ran along the rows of spectators. Dad and I ate the popcorn and peanuts that we had bought. After the ringmaster welcomed us, the circus began.

Almost all of the words that let you see, feel, smell, taste, and hear what was happening are gone. The writer has not used words in a way that helped you use your imagination.

GO ON.

WRITE ABOUT THE THEME: Fossils

There are many mysteries in the world. Scientists spend their lives trying to solve some of these mysteries. One of the best tools for learning about our world is the earth itself. Over time, many different kinds of things have been hidden in the ground. Some scientists spend their whole lives digging in the ground to uncover what is hidden there. These scientists are sometimes called *fossil hunters.* They look for clues about what life was like long ago when dinosaurs roamed Earth.

Consider the following ideas for your piece of writing:

* Write about a time when you or someone you know found a fossil.

* Describe a dinosaur that you have learned about.

* Tell about a time when you or someone you know found something by digging in the ground.

You do not have to use the suggestions shown above. You can use your own idea about **Fossils** for your piece of writing. As you write about the theme, use examples from real life, from what you read or watch, or from your imagination.

Use a separate sheet of paper for listing ideas, organizing your thoughts, or writing a rough draft. You may use the REVISING AND EDITING CHECKLIST on page 6 in this workbook to help you as you work on your draft.

When you are ready, you may begin your draft.

After you have finished your draft, you may use the English/Language Arts Rubric chart on pages 4 and 5 in this workbook to help you as you write your final copy.

GO ON.

Name _____   Date _____

FINAL COPY

Use the English/Language Arts Rubric chart on pages 4 and 5 in this
workbook to check your writing and make changes.

_____

_____

_____

_____

_____

_____

_____

_____

_____

_____

_____

_____

_____

_____

STOP.

PART 2: READING

Tips for Staying with Your First Answer

On a multiple-choice test, the first answer you choose is usually correct. This is true even if you aren't sure which answer is correct.

Read the paragraph below and the question that follows.

> The city of Plainville has just had an election. Jessica Stone was elected mayor. It is her job to represent the city at all public activities. She also has a vote on the city council. There were six people elected to the city council. The members of the council make decisions about taking care of city property. The people who live in Plainville voted in the election. They decided what people were elected. Everyone has a part in the government of the city.

1. Who is responsible for approving the cleanup of city parks?
   A. the mayor
   B. the city council
   C. the voters
   D. the Department of Parks

Notice the words *responsible for approving the cleanup* in the question. These words are not in the paragraph, but they are key words. You need to look for words in the paragraph that mean the same thing as these key words.

- The mayor represents the city and has a vote on the City Council. She cannot approve the clean-up by herself. That makes answer A wrong.
- The city council makes decisions about taking care of city property. That means the same as *approving the cleanup*. Answer B is the best answer so far.
- The voters decided which people were elected. That is not the same as approving the cleanup of parks. That means answer C is wrong.
- The Department of Parks isn't in the paragraph, so answer D is wrong.
- The best answer is B.

If you weren't sure that answer B was right, you might have picked answer D because it had the word *Parks* in it. That's why it is important to stay with your first answer unless you are sure another answer is better.

GO ON.

DIRECTIONS

Read Selection 1. Answer the five multiple-choice questions that follow Selection 1. You may look back at the selection at any time.

Go on to Selection 2. Answer the five multiple-choice questions that follow Selection 2. You may look back at the selection at any time.

Then answer the two multiple-choice questions in the section called PART 2: CROSS-TEXT QUESTIONS.

As you answer the multiple-choice questions, choose the BEST answer. Do not worry if there are questions you cannot answer. Take your time and do as well as you can.

When you have finished reading the selections and answering all of the questions, you may wish to go back and check your work. Do not go on to the next section until you are told to do so.

GO ON.

Clues About the Past

1   Sometimes nature gives us clues about the past. We can learn about what happened long ago by looking at fossils. Fossils are like footprints. We can find footprints in mud, sand, snow, or dirt. Footprints give us an idea about where a person went and how big the person was. In the same way, fossils can tell us a lot about things that lived long ago.

2   Fossils are found in some rocks. Sometimes the fossils are only shapes left in the stone. A part of a plant that lived long ago often leaves its outline. Though the plant dies, we can see the shape of the plant from the outline.

3   Bones are often found buried deep in old rivers. Because they are packed into the dirt or rock, they keep their shape. We can discover shells this way, too. Big bones <u>provide</u> clues about the size of dinosaurs. They are like puzzle pieces. Each piece we find helps us see the picture better.

4   Even footprints can be fossils. When a dinosaur stepped on mud, the tracks stayed. The ground dried. Scientists have found the tracks. The footprints give clues about how dinosaurs walked. Some animals dragged their tails. How do we know this? Scientists have found places where dinosaurs and other animals left their tail prints.

5   Fossils give us clues about animals that are not on Earth today. We can learn about what dinosaurs looked like and how big they were. We can learn about plants and animals that are no longer around. These clues help us solve the mystery of the past.

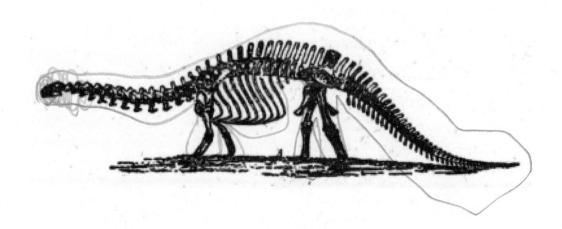

GO ON.

Name _____ Date _____

PART 2: READING SELECTION #1

DIRECTIONS: For each question, circle the BEST answer. You may look back at the selection as often as necessary.

1 In paragraph 3, what does the word *provide* mean?

A. to find

B. to bury

C. to like

D. to give

2 How do footprint fossils help people understand dinosaurs?

A. They show what dinosaurs ate.

B. They show how tall dinosaurs were.

C. They show how high dinosaurs jumped.

D. They show how dinosaurs walked.

3 This story was mainly written to

A. ask readers to look for fossils.

B. explain what readers can learn from fossils.

C. describe how scientists work.

D. make readers afraid of dinosaurs.

GO ON.

Name _____   Date _____

4 Which of these is a fact found in the passage?

A. Scientists love to find fossils.

B. Fossils are found in rock or stone.

C. Finding dinosaur tracks is easy and fun.

D. Dinosaurs are interesting to study.

5 As people find more fossils, scientists will probably

A. discover things they had never learned before.

B. run out of things to learn about.

C. grow tired of studying dinosaurs.

D. try to leave footprints in the mud.

GO ON.

Tracks

1 Following animal tracks is fun. You can see where animals have gone. Dinosaurs left tracks, too. Following them gives us clues about how they lived. Let's follow the tracks of a dinosaur at Rocky Hill, Connecticut. This is where we find Dinosaur State Park.

2 In 1968, workers started to make a building at Rocky Hill. They found tracks where they were going to build. Everyone stopped working. They found more than 2,000 dinosaur tracks. Scientists knew this was important. They did not make the building. They made the place a park, instead. Now people can visit the park to learn about the tracks.

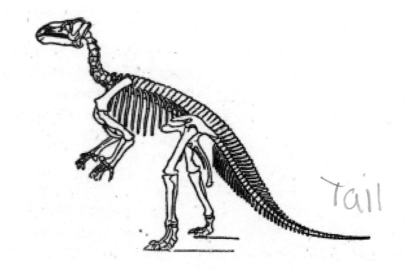

Tail

3   The tracks are from a dinosaur called eubrontes. Scientists didn't find any bones from the dinosaurs that left these tracks. They learned a lot about the dinosaur from the tracks, though. The dinosaur walked on only two feet. Its feet were far apart, but it didn't take very big steps.

4   Scientists compared the tracks at Rocky Hill to the tracks of other dinosaurs. From this they guessed what it looked like. The dinosaur looked a lot like the dinosaur named dilophosaurus (dī-lof´-ə-sor-əs). We know a lot about this dinosaur. It ate meat. It had <u>powerful</u> claws for catching food. The dinosaur was about the weight of a horse. It stood around 8 feet tall.

5   At Dinosaur State Park, there are many things to do. You can even take the tracks home with you! The Park allows visitors to do something called casting. Casting is like copying one of the footprints. Visitors put a metal ring around a track. Then they pour some plaster into the ring. When it dries, the plaster looks like the footprint. After you make the cast, you can take it home.

GO ON.

Name _____ Date _____

PART 2: READING SELECTION #2

DIRECTIONS: For each question, circle the BEST answer. You may look back at the selection as often as necessary.

6 Which of these is true about the dilophosaurus?

A. It liked to swim.

B. It hid in rocks.

C. It lived in China.

D. It ate meat.

7 Why did the people in Rocky Hill cancel plans for a new building?

A. They felt history was more important than a new building.

B. They thought the new building would not look nice.

C. They decided they didn't need any more buildings.

D. They wanted to make a park where children could play.

8 This story would most likely be found in a

A. family newsletter.

B. book of poems.

C. science magazine.

D. storybook.

GO ON.

Name _____ Date _____

9 Look at the following chart.

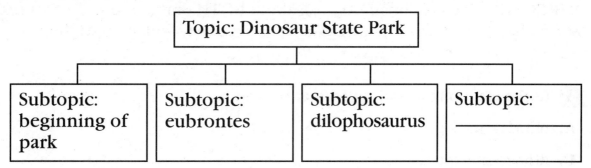

Which of these belongs in the blank space?

A. park schedule

B. casting tracks

C. visitors' center

D. digging bones

10 In paragraph 4, what does the word *powerful* mean?

A. strange

B. sharp

C. strong

D. tiny

GO ON.

Name _____ Date _____

PART 2: CROSS-TEXT QUESTIONS

DIRECTIONS: Questions 11–12 ask about BOTH of the selections you read. For each question, circle the BEST answer. You may look back at the two selections as often as necessary.

11 Both selections contain information about

A. old rivers.

B. dinosaurs.

C. Rocky Hill, Connecticut.

D. plant fossils.

12 Which of these would be a good title for both selections?

A. Living Things of Long Ago

B. A Day at Dinosaur State Park

C. Footprints

D. How to Cast a Fossil

STOP.

PART 2: WRITING IN RESPONSE TO READING

Tips for Using a Web

A web is a type of graphic organizer. It is a good tool when you want to gather information about a topic. It is also useful when you are gathering facts to support an opinion.

Below is an example of a web. It shows some facts that Carl collected. The center of the web is a Carl's opinion. It will also be the main idea of his paragraph. There are five squares connected to the center square. These are the facts that support Carl's opinion. Each of them will be a sentence in his paragraph.

Use a web to help you gather information. Then use the notes you make on the web when you do the first draft of your writing.

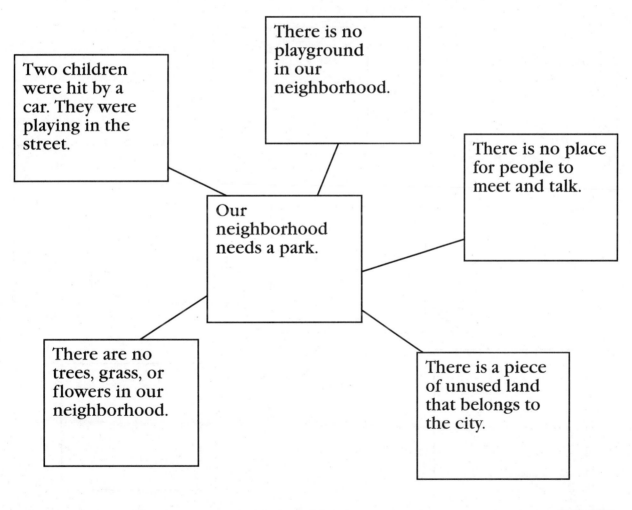

GO ON.

PART 2: WRITING IN RESPONSE TO READING

DIRECTIONS: Think about the information you learned in the selections you just read. Then answer the following question.

Do you think people can learn about life long ago from studying fossils?

Decide whether your answer to the question above is YES or NO. Write your opinion in the center square. Think carefully about each selection. Use the other squares to write down any facts that you find that support your opinion. Use the information you have gathered on the web to answer the question above. Remember to use details and examples from "Clues About the Past" and "Tracks."

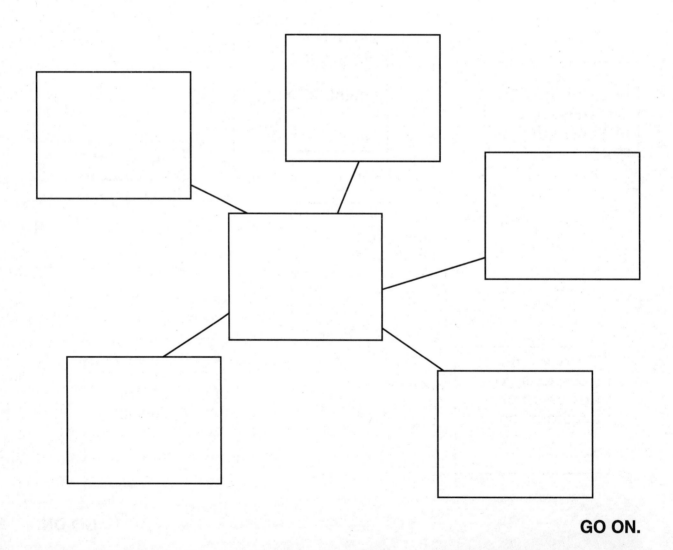

GO ON.

Name _____   Date _____

DRAFT

Remember to refer to the Revising and Editing Checklist on page 6 in this workbook as you develop your draft.

_____

_____

_____

_____

_____

_____

_____

_____

_____

_____

_____

_____

_____

_____

GO ON.

Name _____ Date _____

FINAL COPY

Use the English/Language Arts Rubric chart on pages 4 and 5 in this workbook to check your writing and make changes.

_____

_____

_____

_____

_____

_____

_____

_____

_____

_____

_____

_____

_____

_____

STOP.

PART 1: WRITING FROM KNOWLEDGE AND EXPERIENCE

This test is divided into two parts that are all linked to one theme or important idea. The theme for this unit is **Fossils.** Keep the theme in mind as you are taking this test.

In Part 1, you will be presented with a number of ways to write about the theme. You must choose ONLY ONE way. After you have finished reading the information provided, begin writing a draft. When you have completed your draft, use the REVISING AND EDITING CHECKLIST on page 6 in this workbook to review your writing. Then enter your final copy on the page marked FINAL COPY. You may use a dictionary, thesaurus, grammar book, or spelling book for Part 1 writing.

GO ON.

WRITE ABOUT THE THEME: Fossils

Scientists who hunt for fossils and dinosaur bones lead exciting lives. Their work takes them all over the world. They search in mountains and in deserts. Sometimes they have to look for a long time before they find anything. Scientists have to be very patient. They also have to spend a lot of time in places where there are no soft beds or hot meals. The most important thing in their lives is the hunt for that perfect fossil or maybe even the bones of an entire dinosaur. Does that kind of life appeal to you?

Consider the following ideas for your piece of writing:

• Write about whether or not you would like to be a scientist like the ones in the paragraph above.

• Describe what you think it would be like to go on a fossil hunt in the desert.

• Tell about a time when someone you know or have read about discovered a fossil.

You do not have to use the suggestions shown above. You can use your own idea about **Fossils** for your piece of writing. As you write about the theme, use examples from real life, from what you read or watch, or from your imagination.

Use a separate sheet of paper for listing ideas, organizing your thoughts, or writing a rough draft. You may use the REVISING AND EDITING CHECKLIST on page 6 in this workbook to help you as you work on your draft.

When you are ready, you may begin your draft.

After you have finished your draft, you may use the English/Language Arts Rubric chart on pages 4 and 5 in this workbook to help you as you write your final copy.

GO ON.

Name _____   Date _____

FINAL COPY

Use the English/Language Arts Rubric chart on pages 4 and 5 in this workbook to check your writing and make changes.

_____

_____

_____

_____

_____

_____

_____

_____

_____

_____

_____

_____

STOP.

PART 2: READING

DIRECTIONS

Read Selection 1. Answer the five multiple-choice questions that follow Selection 1. You may look back at the selection at any time.

Go on to Selection 2. Answer the five multiple-choice questions that follow Selection 2. You may look back at the selection at any time.

Then answer the two multiple-choice questions in the section called PART 2: CROSS-TEXT QUESTIONS.

As you answer the multiple-choice questions, choose the BEST answer. Do not worry if there are questions you cannot answer. Take your time and do as well as you can.

When you have finished reading the selections and answering all of the questions, you may wish to go back and check your work. Do not go on to the next section until you are told to do so.

GO ON.

Dinosaur Monument

1   Allie looked out the back window. The trees whizzed by. Allie shouted, "Elk! Elk!" Her cousin Jake placed a mark by the word *elk* on his paper. In their one-hour car trip, they had seen three elk, one eagle, and two rabbits.

2   Allie, Jake, and their families were going to Colorado's Dinosaur National Monument. Allie had never been there before. Jake couldn't wait to show her around.

3   They made their first stop. Allie was surprised. She thought they might see big statues. That's what she thought monuments were. What she saw was a huge cliff. Down below was the Yampa River.

4   Everyone got out of the car. Jake started to look very closely at the ground. "Are we still playing the animal game?" Allie asked.

5   "You could say that. I'm looking for fossils," Jake said. Allie had learned about fossils in school. She thought that only scientists could find fossils. They walked for a long time. They looked at the cliff. They looked at the ground. She learned that the monument didn't have statues. It was a place where a lot of dinosaur bones had been found.

6   Their parents told them it was time to go. Next they visited a rock quarry. They crossed the border of Colorado. Now they were in Utah. The quarry was very, very deep. People were looking for fossils there, too.

7   "Since 1915, people have been finding dinosaur fossils here," Jake's mother told them.

8   Then they came to the museum. They saw <u>gigantic</u> bones. Some were as tall as Allie was. It helped her think about what dinosaurs must have looked like.

9   Jake asked his mother if he and Allie could go outside. For two hours they hunted for fossils. Allie became bored. She wondered if there were really fossils here.

10   At last Jake cried, "Over here!"

11   Allie ran to Jake. She saw a rock on the ground. "I don't see anything," Allie said. Jake picked up the rock. "It's a tooth. Look at the shape."

12   Allie couldn't believe it. They found a fossil! She was ready to stay for the whole day and look for more.

GO ON.

Name _____ Date _____

PART 2: READING SELECTION #1

DIRECTIONS: For each question, circle the BEST answer. You may look back at the selection as often as necessary.

1 Jake could not wait to show Allie around the monument because

A. he wanted to continue their game.

B. she had never been there before.

C. he wanted to show her a big statue.

D. he was excited to show her the cliff.

2 Allie wanted to stay at the rock quarry because she

A. loved being with her mother.

B. enjoyed being outside.

C. was excited about finding a fossil.

D. was tired of riding in the car.

3 This story is mostly about a

A. girl who visits her cousin.

B. girl who visits a dinosaur park.

C. family that goes hiking for the day.

D. boy who wanders off without his parents.

GO ON.

Name _____   Date _____

4 Look at the character web.

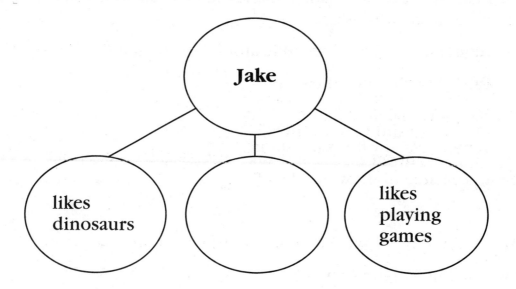

Which of these belongs in the empty circle?

A. likes exploring

B. likes looking at statues

C. likes hunting elk

D. likes collecting rocks

5 In paragraph 8, what does the word *gigantic* mean?

A. dinosaur

B. large

C. hard

D. straight

GO ON.

Lynnosaurus

1   Joey and his aunt walked along the boardwalk. Aunt Lynn bought Joey an ice-cream cone. Joey was glad to be with his aunt.

2   Aunt Lynn had left two months ago to visit Australia. Joey had missed Aunt Lynn. She had promised to come back and tell him about her trip. Now Joey had many questions for her.

3   "What did you do there?" Joey asked.

4   "I went on a dinosaur dig," she said. Joey couldn't believe it.

5   "Wow," he said. "Did you find any dinosaurs?"

6   "No, but I found three fossils in Dinosaur Cove."

7   As they walked to the water, Aunt Lynn talked about her first dig. "Dinosaur Cove is on the ocean. It was windy. My friends and I began to dig in the sand. We dug for the whole day. Our hole was very deep. We didn't find anything."

8   "That must have been no fun," Joey said.

Scientists thought the bone might be from a dinosaur's leg.

9 "You are right. It was also wet. As the sun set, we became cold. But we knew that hundreds of fossils had been found there. We were <u>determined</u>. We kept going."

10 Then Aunt Lynn told about the first fossil they found. It was three weeks after they started. "We were tired. We almost went home. We started digging in our third hole. After an hour, I hit something. I was so excited, I started to shake! We all started to dig around it. The bone was about as long as your arm. It was as wide as my wrist!"

11 Joey asked if she had pictures. She had taken four whole rolls of film. As they looked at the pictures, she told more stories. She had to come home before they knew what kind of dinosaur they had found. Scientists were studying the bone right now. They thought it might be from a dinosaur's leg.

12 "Will they name a dinosaur after you?" Joey asked.

13 "I never thought about it. If you ever hear of a lynnosaurus, you'll know what I found," she said. They laughed as they wandered back to the car.

GO ON.

Name _____   Date _____

PART 2: READING SELECTION #2

DIRECTIONS: For each question, circle the BEST answer. You may look back at the selection as often as necessary.

6 In paragraph 9, what does the word *determined* mean?

A. feeling a little sad

B. not giving up

C. keeping quiet

D. trying to get warm

7 What is this story MOSTLY about?

A. A woman shows a boy pictures.

B. A boy gets ice cream on the boardwalk.

C. A woman and her friends dig a deep hole.

D. An aunt talks to her nephew about a trip.

8 Aunt Lynn laughed at the end of the story because

A. Joey had ice cream on his nose.

B. she was looking at a silly picture she took.

C. a dinosaur that had her name sounded funny.

D. Joey told a funny joke.

GO ON.

Name _____   Date _____

9 Aunt Lynn probably likes to

A. study dinosaurs.

B. go jogging in the morning.

C. build sandcastles in the sand.

D. watch people on the beach.

10 Aunt Lynn went to Australia to

A. dig for dinosaur fossils.

B. look for seashells.

C. surf in the ocean.

D. take pictures of the beach.

GO ON.

Name _____ Date _____

PART 2: CROSS-TEXT QUESTIONS

DIRECTIONS: Questions 11–12 ask about BOTH of the selections you read. For each question, circle the BEST answer. You may look back at the two selections as often as necessary.

11 What is one way that both of these selections are alike?

A. They are both articles.

B. They are both poems.

C. They are both biographies.

D. They are both stories.

12 What is another way that both of these selections are alike?

A. The people in each selection are related to each other.

B. Both selections take place at the beach.

C. All of the people in both selections are adults.

D. Both selections have surprise endings.

STOP.

PART 2: WRITING IN RESPONSE TO READING

DIRECTIONS: Think about the people and their activities in the selections you just read. Then answer the following question.

Do you think that only scientists can be fossil hunters?

Think carefully about the question. Then think about each selection. You may wish to use a graphic organizer to collect information from the selections that you think will support your answer. Decide whether your answer to the question above is YES or NO. Then explain your answer by using specific examples and details from "Dinosaur Monument" and "Lynnosaurus."

GO ON.

Name _____   Date _____

FINAL COPY

Use the English/Language Arts Rubric chart on pages 4 and 5 in this
workbook to check your writing and make changes.

_____

_____

_____

_____

_____

_____

_____

_____

_____

_____

_____

_____

_____

STOP.

_____

PART 1: WRITING FROM KNOWLEDGE AND EXPERIENCE

This test is divided into two parts that are all linked to one theme or important idea. The theme for this unit is **Courage.** Refer to the Theme Connections pages at the end of each selection in Unit 5 in your Student Anthology for additional information about the theme. Keep the theme in mind as you are taking this test.

In Part 1, you will be presented with a number of ways to write about the theme. You must choose ONLY ONE way. After you have finished reading the information provided, begin writing a draft. When you have completed your draft, use the REVISING AND EDITING CHECKLIST on page 6 in this workbook to review your writing. Then enter your final copy on the page marked FINAL COPY. You may use a dictionary, thesaurus, grammar book, or spelling book for Part 1 writing.

Tips for Traits of Good Writing
Improving Sentence Fluency in Writing

For more information on the traits of good writing, turn to page 13 in the *Open Court Reading Language Arts Handbook*.

Sentence fluency makes your writing more interesting for your readers. Your sentences should flow like the sentences you use when you speak. You can make your writing flow more smoothly by using different kinds of sentences. If you use all short sentences, your writing will not flow. If you use all long sentences, your writing will not flow. Try to use a mixture of long and short sentences. Your writing will be smoother and easier to understand.

GO ON.

Read the paragraph below. As you read, notice the mixture of long and short sentences that the writer uses.

> My walk home from school is easy. I go through the school playground and walk to Elm Street. At the corner of Elm and Spring, I turn left. I walk three blocks. When I get to Hanover Avenue, I turn right. My house is the third one from the corner. I'm home in ten minutes.

The paragraph above has sentences that flow. When you read the sentences aloud or to yourself, they flow together smoothly. The mixture of long and short sentences gives the writing a pleasing rhythm.

Check for sentence fluency when you are revising the first draft of your writing. Check the pattern of your sentences. All long sentences or all short sentences do not create smooth writing. Make sure that your writing has some of both.

GO ON.

WRITE ABOUT THE THEME: Courage

What do you think of when you hear the word *courage?* Does someone who faces danger have courage? Does a person who risks his or her life to save another person have courage? Do you have courage? Before you answer the last question, think about what the word means. Courage is the ability to face fear. Being afraid does not mean you do not have courage. It is natural for humans to have fears. You have courage if you don't let your fears keep you from doing what you want to do or what you know is right.

Consider the following ideas for your piece of writing:

- Write about a time when you or someone you know showed courage.

- Tell about a time when people worked together to do something courageous.

- Describe a famous person who has shown courage.

You do not have to use the suggestions shown above. You can use your own idea about **Courage** for your piece of writing. As you write about the theme, use examples from real life, from what you read or watch, or from your imagination.

Use a separate sheet of paper for listing ideas, organizing your thoughts, or writing a rough draft. You may use the REVISING AND EDITING CHECKLIST on page 6 in this workbook to help you as you work on your draft.

When you are ready, you may begin your draft.

After you have finished your draft, you may use the English/Language Arts Rubric chart on pages 4 and 5 in this workbook to help you as you write your final copy.

GO ON.

Name _____   Date _____

FINAL COPY

Use the English/Language Arts Rubric chart on pages 4 and 5 in this workbook to check your writing and make changes.

_____

_____

_____

_____

_____

_____

_____

_____

_____

_____

_____

_____

STOP.

PART 2: READING

Tips for Eliminating Incorrect Answer Choices

On a multiple-choice test, sometimes you know that an answer choice is not right. When that happens, eliminate that answer choice right away. It will be easier for you to find the correct answer because you have one less answer to choose from.

Read the paragraphs below and answer the question that follows.

The world's largest desert is the Sahara. It is located in the northern part of Africa. Parts of the Sahara are large hills of sand. Other parts of the desert have miles of huge stones. There are also mountains of rock with nothing growing on them. There are some plants in most parts of the desert, but they don't grow very well. There isn't enough water.

It can get very hot and very cold in some parts of the Sahara. In the summer, temperatures during the day can be 130 degrees. After sunset on the same day, the temperature can drop to freezing.

1. Which of the following statements is TRUE?
   A. The Sahara Desert is located in the northern part of Asia.
   B. There are plants in all parts of the Sahara Desert.
   C. The Sahara is the world's largest desert.
   D. The Sahara Desert does not have extreme temperatures.

Look at the answer choices.
- You can eliminate choice A. The second sentence of the first paragraph tells you the desert is in Africa.

- You can also eliminate choice B. The first paragraph tells you that there are mountains of rock with nothing growing on them.

- Choice C is probably the right answer. The first sentence of the first paragraph says that it is the world's largest desert. Because you could eliminate choices A and B, you have to decide between choices C and D.

- Because the second paragraph says that the desert gets very hot and very cold, choice D is not correct.

- Choice C must be the right answer.

GO ON.

DIRECTIONS

Read Selection 1. Answer the five multiple-choice questions that follow Selection 1. You may look back at the selection at any time.

Go on to Selection 2. Answer the five multiple-choice questions that follow Selection 2. You may look back at the selection at any time.

Then answer the two multiple-choice questions in the section called PART 2: CROSS-TEXT QUESTIONS.

As you answer the multiple-choice questions, choose the BEST answer. Do not worry if there are questions you cannot answer. Take your time and do as well as you can.

When you have finished reading the selections and answering all of the questions, you may wish to go back and check your work. Do not go on to the next section until you are told to do so.

GO ON.

New Home

1 The first day in my new home was exciting. It was also a little scary. A big man and a little girl took me away from the barn where I was born. At first I was sad. But the little girl held me and petted me. It felt good. I purred a lot. The big man smiled, so I said, "Meow."

2 We went for a ride in a car. I had never been in a car before. I saw lots of trees and houses. Then the little girl took me inside a house. A nice woman held me and petted me.

3 "Welcome to your new home!" she said. She put me down on the floor. The little girl gave me a bowl of water and some food. I had a snack and a drink. Then I went exploring.

4   The house was so big! There were lots of places to hide and play. I had fun looking around. Then I found a very scary thing. A dog was <u>curled up</u> on a pillow. The dog was sleeping. I was afraid of him. But I wanted him to like me.

5   Slowly I crept up to the big dog. I sniffed his nose. He opened his eyes. I didn't know what to do. Then the dog did a strange thing. He licked me! I started to purr. Now we are best friends. I love my new family, especially the dog.

GO ON.

Name _____ Date _____

PART 2: READING SELECTION #1

DIRECTIONS: For each question, circle the BEST answer. You may look back at the selection as often as necessary.

1 In paragraph 4, what does *curled up* mean?

A. snacking

B. snoring

C. snuggling

D. stretching

2 Who is telling this story?

A. a big man

B. a little girl

C. a dog

D. a kitten

3 Where did the girl get her new pet?

A. at a pet store

B. at the next-door neighbor's

C. from a barn

D. near a grocery store

GO ON.

Name _____ Date _____

4 Which of these BEST describes the pet's new home?

A. dark

B. friendly

C. scary

D. small

5 Why does the kitten purr in this story?

A. The kitten is curious.

B. The kitten is tired.

C. The kitten is happy.

D. The kitten is hungry.

GO ON.

The Dumplings and the Dragon

1   Long ago in Japan there lived an old man and his wife. One morning the old woman went to the river. She saw a peach floating in the water. She picked it up. A baby boy fell out! The old man and woman named him Momo. This means "Little Peach."

2   Momo grew up to be strong and brave. He loved the old man and woman. One day he said, "I will battle the dragon over the mountain. I will give all of his gold to you and the other people in the village."

3   The old woman said, "Be careful, my son. Take these tasty <u>dumplings</u> with you." Momo put the dumplings in his pocket.

4   On the trip, Momo met a monkey. Momo gave him a tasty dumpling. The monkey followed him.

Soon they heard a bird call. Momo gave the bird a dumpling. The bird followed them. Soon they saw a dog on the road. Momo gave the dog a dumpling. Then the dog joined the group.

5 Finally they came to the dragon's castle. The bird flew over the castle gate. He said the dragon was asleep. The monkey climbed over the castle wall and opened the gate. Momo and the dog fought the dragon. The dragon ran away.

6 Momo took the dragon's gold home. He gave some to the old man and woman. He gave the rest of it to the other villagers. Everyone lived in happiness and comfort for the rest of their lives.

GO ON.

Name _____ Date _____

PART 2: READING SELECTION #2

DIRECTIONS: For each question, circle the BEST answer. You may look back at the selection as often as necessary.

6 The reader can tell that *dumplings* are a kind of

A. tool.

B. food.

C. gold.

D. note.

7 Which of these words does NOT describe Momo?

A. funny

B. brave

C. giving

D. strong

8 This story could BEST be described as

A. a folktale.

B. science fiction.

C. a mystery.

D. a biography.

GO ON.

Name _____ Date _____

9 Look at this chart with events from the story.

1	Momo meets a bird.
2	Momo meets a dog.
3	Momo meets a monkey.
4	Momo fights a dragon.

Which choice shows the correct order of events?

A. 2, 3, 1, 4

B. 3, 2, 1, 4

C. 3, 1, 2, 4

D. 1, 2, 3, 4

10 What most helps Momo defeat the dragon?

A. weapons

B. teamwork

C. dumplings

D. peaches

GO ON.

PART 2: CROSS-TEXT QUESTIONS

DIRECTIONS: Questions 11–12 ask about BOTH of the selections you read. For each question, circle the BEST answer. You may look back at the two selections as often as necessary.

11 Which of the following statements is TRUE?

A. Both selections take place in Japan.

B. There is a dragon in both selections.

C. There are animals in both selections.

D. There is a little girl in both selections.

12 In both selections, the main characters

A. had to fight to get what they wanted.

B. showed courage when they faced possible danger.

C. found a treasure and shared it.

D. lived in a barn.

STOP.

PART 2: WRITING IN RESPONSE TO READING

Tips for Using a Venn Diagram

A Venn diagram is a type of graphic organizer. You can use it to do some planning before you begin to write. A Venn diagram is helpful when you want to show how two things are alike and different. The Venn diagram has a place for you to write how the two things are different. It also has a place for you to write how the two things are alike.

Below is an example of a Venn diagram. It shows some of the ways that two animals are alike and different. The information in the left side of the diagram tells ways that a whale is different from an elephant. The information in the right side of the diagram tells ways that an elephant is different from a whale. The information in the middle tells how whales and elephants are alike.

Use a Venn diagram to help you gather and organize information. Then use the information from the Venn diagram when you do the first draft of your writing.

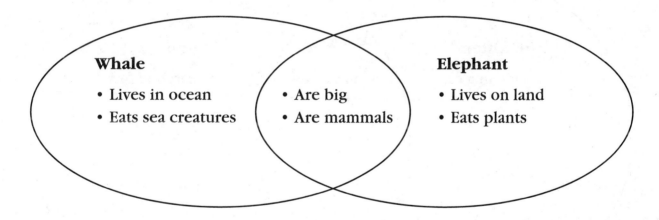

Whale
- Lives in ocean
- Eats sea creatures

- Are big
- Are mammals

Elephant
- Lives on land
- Eats plants

GO ON.

PART 2: WRITING IN RESPONSE TO READING

Think about the information you learned in the selections you just read. Then answer the following question.

Do you think that there is more than one way to show courage?

Think about the first selection. Use the left side of the Venn diagram below to list ways that the kitten's courage in "New Home" was different from Momo's courage. Then think about the second selection. Use the right side of the Venn diagram to list ways that Momo's courage in "The Dumplings and the Dragon" was different from the kitten's courage. In the center of the Venn diagram, list the ways that the courage shown in both selections was alike. Using the notes from the Venn diagram, decide whether your answer to the question above is YES or NO. Then explain your answer by using specific examples and details from "New Home" and "The Dumplings and the Dragon."

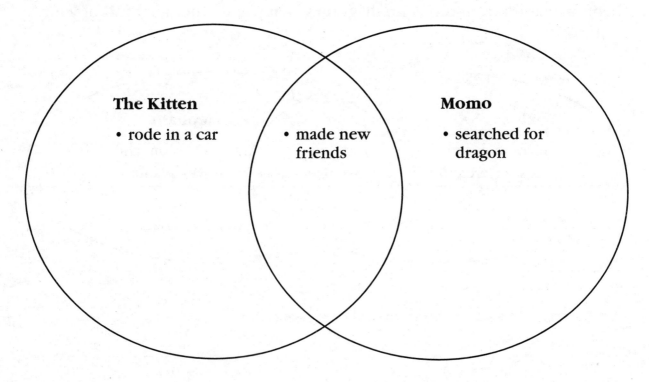

The Kitten
- rode in a car

- made new friends

Momo
- searched for dragon

GO ON.

Name _____   Date _____

DRAFT

Remember to refer to the Revising and Editing Checklist on page 6 in this
workbook as you develop your draft.

_____

_____

_____

_____

_____

_____

_____

_____

_____

_____

_____

_____

_____

GO ON.

Name _____   Date _____

FINAL COPY

Use the English/Language Arts Rubric chart on pages 4 and 5 in this
workbook to check your writing and make changes.

_____

_____

_____

_____

_____

_____

_____

_____

_____

_____

_____

STOP.

PART 1: WRITING FROM KNOWLEDGE AND EXPERIENCE

This test is divided into two parts that are all linked to one theme or important idea. The theme for this unit is **Courage.** Keep the theme in mind as you are taking this test.

In Part 1, you will be presented with a number of ways to write about the theme. You must choose ONLY ONE way. After you have finished reading the information provided, begin writing a draft. When you have completed your draft, use the REVISING AND EDITING CHECKLIST on page 6 in this workbook to review your writing. Then enter your final copy on the page marked FINAL COPY. You may use a dictionary, thesaurus, grammar book, or spelling book for Part 1 writing.

GO ON.

WRITE ABOUT THE THEME: Courage

Courage can be expressed in many ways. It takes courage to try something new. It takes courage to move to a new place. It takes courage to keep trying when you're not succeeding. Sometimes it takes courage to decide not to do something. All of these examples are part of everyday life. They are part of your life. In what ways do you show courage?

Consider the following ideas for your piece of writing:

- Write about a time when you or someone you know had the courage to try something new.

- Tell about a time when you or someone you know had the courage to decide not to do something.

- Explain how you or someone you know had the courage to go to a new school or move to a new neighborhood.

You do not have to use the suggestions shown above. You can use your own idea about **Courage** for your piece of writing. As you write about the theme, use examples from real life, from what you read or watch, or from your imagination.

Use a separate sheet of paper for listing ideas, organizing your thoughts, or writing a rough draft. You may use the REVISING AND EDITING CHECKLIST on page 6 in this workbook to help you as you work on your draft.

When you are ready, you may begin your draft.

After you have finished your draft, you may use the English/Language Arts Rubric chart on pages 4 and 5 in this workbook to help you as you write your final copy.

GO ON.

Name _____   Date _____

FINAL COPY

Use the English/Language Arts Rubric chart on pages 4 and 5 in this workbook to check your writing and make changes.

_____

_____

_____

_____

_____

_____

_____

_____

_____

_____

_____

_____

_____

_____

STOP.

PART 2: READING

DIRECTIONS

Read Selection 1. Answer the five multiple-choice questions that follow Selection 1. You may look back at the selection at any time.

Go on to Selection 2. Answer the five multiple-choice questions that follow Selection 2. You may look back at the selection at any time.

Then answer the two multiple-choice questions in the section called PART 2: CROSS-TEXT QUESTIONS.

As you answer the multiple-choice questions, choose the BEST answer. Do not worry if there are questions you cannot answer. Take your time and do as well as you can.

When you have finished reading the selections and answering all of the questions, you may wish to go back and check your work. Do not go on to the next section until you are told to do so.

GO ON.

Tryout

1 Hanna loved to act. She and her friend, Ally, wanted to be famous movie stars when they grew up.

2 One day, Ally came to Hanna's house. "The high school is doing a play," she said. "They need kids our age to try out. I think we should do it."

3 "A real play!" Hanna said. Then a wave of fear came over her. "I couldn't try out in front of people," she said. "I would be too scared."

4 "We can do it," Ally said. "It will be lots of fun. You'll see."

5 The day of the tryouts came. Hanna and Ally went to the high school. Dozens of children were there. Hanna felt cold and hot at the same time. She was very scared. "I can do this," she said to herself. "I might even become a star."

6   Finally it was her turn to try out. Three grown-ups were sitting at a table. They listened to Hanna read. They asked her a lot of questions. One told her to pretend to paint a house. Hanna felt scared inside. But she did everything they asked.

7   Tryouts lasted all day. Hanna and Ally waited until everyone was finished. Finally, the grown-ups handed out a list of names. Hanna's name was on the list. Ally's name was there, too. They both had <u>made the play</u>!

8   "Maybe I'll be a famous star after all," Hanna thought.

GO ON.

Name _____   Date _____

PART 2: READING SELECTION #1

DIRECTIONS: For each question, circle the BEST answer. You may look back at the selection as often as necessary.

1 Which of these BEST describes how Ally felt?

A. shy about acting

B. worried for Hanna

C. excited to try out

D. afraid to try out

2 The reader can tell that the tryouts were probably held

A. on a school day.

B. on a Saturday.

C. during a school night.

D. during the summer.

3 In paragraph 7, what does *made the play* mean?

A. finished the play

B. wrote the play

C. would be in the play

D. would see the play

GO ON.

Name _____   Date _____

4 Look at the plot diagram.

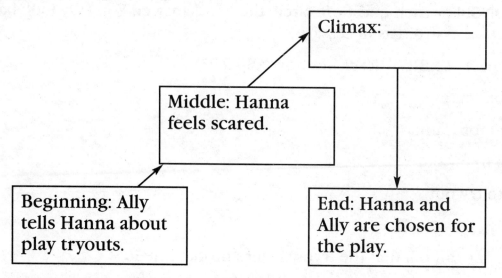

Which of these BEST completes the diagram?

A. Three grown-ups ask questions.

B. Hanna tries out for the play.

C. Hanna answers questions.

D. Hanna and Ally wait for the list.

5 How will Hanna probably feel just before the play begins?

A. scared

B. cheerful

C. sorry

D. tired

GO ON.

A Special Hike

1   Mari was from New York City. She was visiting her favorite relatives in Colorado. Uncle Will had decided to take the family on a hike in Mesa Verde National Park. Mari looked at the rocky trail. She had never been on a hike before.

2   Uncle Will saw her face. He smiled and took her hand. "It's not as hard as it looks," he said. "Besides, there is a special place I want to show you."

3   Soon the family was hiking up the trail. The sun was hot. Strange noises made Mari jump. She wanted to go home. But she knew that Uncle Will would be disappointed.

4   "Not too much farther now," Uncle Will said.

5 Finally they came to the end of the trail. Tall canyon walls stood in front of them. The sun made the canyons look red and gold. Mari had never seen anything so beautiful.

6 She noticed that large <u>dwellings</u> were built into the canyon walls. "What is that?" she asked.

7 "Our Native American ancestors used to live there," Uncle Will said. "They built those cliff dwellings hundreds of years ago. Today we visit their homes to remember them."

8 Mari thought of the people who used to live in the cliff dwellings. She was glad that she had found the courage to finish the hike. She felt proud that she was a Native American. Her people had made the wonderful cliff houses.

GO ON.

Name _____ Date _____

PART 2: READING SELECTION #2

DIRECTIONS: For each question, circle the BEST answer. You may look back at the selection as often as necessary.

6 In paragraph 6, what does the word *dwellings* mean?

A. hills

B. forts

C. homes

D. trails

7 How does Mari feel about the hike at first?

A. excited

B. curious

C. bored

D. worried

8 You can tell that Mari's ancestors were

A. from another country.

B. Native Americans.

C. hikers.

D. from New York.

GO ON.

Name _____ Date _____

9 This story probably takes place during the

A. winter.

B. spring.

C. summer.

D. fall.

10 Mari is doing all of these for the first time EXCEPT

A. meeting her Colorado relatives.

B. seeing cliff dwellings.

C. going on a hike.

D. seeing Mesa Verde National Park.

GO ON.

Name _____ Date _____

PART 2: CROSS-TEXT QUESTIONS

DIRECTIONS: Questions 11–12 ask about BOTH of the selections you read. For each question, circle the BEST answer. You may look back at the two selections as often as necessary.

11 Which of the following statements is TRUE?

A. Both selections are stories.

B. Both selections are biographies

C. Both selections are articles.

D. Both selections are plays.

12 A good title for both selections is

A. The School Play.

B. Danger on the Trail.

C. Becoming a Star.

D. Overcoming Fear.

STOP.

PART 2: WRITING IN RESPONSE TO READING

Think about the characters and their activities in the selections you just read. Then answer the following question.

Do you think that being courageous can change a person?

Think about the main character in each selection. You may wish to use a two-column chart to list the ways that being courageous affected Hanna and Mari. Decide whether your answer to the question above is YES or NO. Then explain your answer, using specific examples and details from "Tryout" and "A Special Hike."

GO ON.

Name _____   Date _____

FINAL COPY

Use the English/Language Arts Rubric chart on pages 4 and 5 in this workbook to check your writing and make changes.

_____

_____

_____

_____

_____

_____

_____

_____

_____

_____

_____

_____

STOP.

PART 1: WRITING FROM KNOWLEDGE AND EXPERIENCE

This test is divided into two parts that are all linked to one theme or important idea. The theme for this unit is **Our Country and Its People.** Refer to the Theme Connections pages at the end of each selection in Unit 6 in your Student Anthology for additional information about the theme. Keep the theme in mind as you are taking this test.

In Part 1, you will be presented with a number of ways to write about the theme. You must choose ONLY ONE way. After you have finished reading the information provided, begin writing a draft. When you have completed your draft, use the REVISING AND EDITING CHECKLIST on page 6 in this workbook to review your writing. Then enter your final copy on the page marked FINAL COPY. You may use a dictionary, thesaurus, grammar book, or spelling book for Part 1 writing.

Tips for Traits of Good Writing
Improving Conventions in Writing

For more information on the traits of good writing, turn to page 13 in the *Open Court Reading Language Arts Handbook*.

Writing that has mistakes confuses a reader. Mistakes stop the flow of the writing. The reader stops thinking about the ideas and starts thinking about the mistakes. Conventions are rules for good writing. There are spelling and grammar conventions. There are capitalization and punctuation conventions. It is important to look for and correct mistakes in your writing. Writing that has no mistakes is a pleasure to read.

GO ON.

Read the following paragraph. It will not be easy to read. The writer didn't check for mistakes.

> Last night I had a great dream I was flying a big plane below me was a bright blue ocean. I think it was the pacifik ocean it was a butaful sight. I landed on an island it had palm trees and coconuts. The people were very friendly. When my dad woke me up he said that I was smiling.

Did you notice that the paragraph was difficult to read? It has spelling, punctuation, and capitalization mistakes. Now read the same paragraph with all the mistakes fixed. Notice how much easier it is to read.

> Last night I had a great dream. I was flying a big plane. Below me was a bright blue ocean. I think it was the Pacific Ocean. It was a beautiful sight. I landed on an island. It had palm trees and coconuts. The people were very friendly. When my dad woke me up, he said that I was smiling.

Always check your writing for mistakes before you share it with readers. Use a dictionary or grammar book to help you make the corrections. Your readers will thank you.

GO ON.

WRITE ABOUT THE THEME: Our Country and Its People

If you have ever moved, you know that it changed your life. Even if you just move from one neighborhood to another, things change. For people who move from one country to another, the changes are very big. The language, climate, and food may be different. That's a lot of change. What makes people willing to change their lives by moving to another country? How long does it take before they begin to feel at home?

Consider the following ideas for your piece of writing:

• Write about a time when you, or someone you know, moved to a new neighborhood.

• Write about a person you know who has moved to the United States from another country.

• Tell about a time when a new student came to your school.

You do not have to use the suggestions shown above. You can use your own idea about **Our Country and Its People** for your piece of writing. As you write about the theme, use examples from real life, from what you read or watch, or from your imagination.

Use a separate sheet of paper for listing ideas, organizing your thoughts, or writing a rough draft. You may use the REVISING AND EDITING CHECKLIST on page 6 in this workbook to help you as you work on your draft.

After you have finished your draft, you may use the English/Language Arts Rubric chart on pages 4 and 5 in this workbook to help you as you write your final copy.

GO ON.

Name _____   Date _____

FINAL COPY

Use the English/Language Arts Rubric chart on pages 4 and 5 in this workbook to check your writing and make changes.

_____

_____

_____

_____

_____

_____

_____

_____

_____

_____

_____

_____

STOP.

PART 2: READING

Tips for Finding Details

On a multiple-choice test, sometimes you are asked about a detail in a story or article. Questions about details are usually about people, places, things, events, or numbers. The answers to detail questions are always in the story or article. Read the paragraph below.

> The lion is known as the king of beasts. Male lions have a mane. It makes them look majestic. An average male weighs 450 pounds. Females weigh less than 300 pounds. Most lions are a light yellow-brown color. Lions are meat eaters. They feed on several animals including zebra, buffalo, wild hogs, birds, and hares. Lions live in the wild for about 15 years.

Now read this question.

Which of the following is a detail from the paragraph?
A. An average male weighs 600 pounds.
B. Lions are plant eaters.
C. Lions live in groups called prides.
D. Most lions are a light, yellow-brown color.

This is how to find the answer. Carefully compare each answer choice to the paragraph.

- The paragraph does not say that an average male weighs 600 pounds. Answer A is wrong.
- The paragraph says that lions eat meat. This makes answer B wrong.
- Even though lions live in prides, it is not mentioned in the paragraph. Answer C is wrong.
- Answer D is right. The sixth sentence in the paragraph says that most lions are a light, yellow-brown color.

GO ON.

DIRECTIONS

Read Selection 1. Answer the five multiple-choice questions that follow Selection 1. You may look back at the selection at any time.

Go on to Selection 2. Answer the five multiple-choice questions that follow Selection 2. You may look back at the selection at any time.

Then answer the two multiple-choice questions in the section called PART 2: CROSS-TEXT QUESTIONS.

As you answer the multiple-choice questions, choose the BEST answer. Do not worry if there are questions you cannot answer. Take your time and do as well as you can.

When you have finished reading the selections and answering all of the questions, you may wish to go back and check your work. Do not go on to the next section until you are told to do so.

GO ON.

Why They Came

1   The United States is filled with immigrants. They came here from around the world. Long ago, most immigrants <u>settled</u> in big cities such as New York City and Philadelphia. Others found homes in different parts of the country.

2   Hundreds of years ago, immigrants came to the United States to find good farmland. Immigrants from Scotland and Ireland settled in southern states such as North Carolina, Georgia, and Alabama. Swedish immigrants found good farmland in western states such as North Dakota and Minnesota. These states had weather like their home countries.

Many immigrants came to America to find land they could farm.

3 German immigrants were also looking for a place to start new lives. The rolling hills of Pennsylvania looked very good to them. They became successful farmers. Today many Pennsylvania farm families have German names.

4 Years ago, Chinese immigrants moved to the western United States. They often came to work on the railroads. Today many cities have neighborhoods filled with the descendents of these immigrants. People like to visit these neighborhoods because they seem like faraway places.

5 Some immigrants came to the United States because the government in their own country changed. The new government rulers made life hard for people. Many Cubans moved to Miami, Florida, because of the government in Cuba. Years ago, many Russians came to this country because of problems in their home country.

6 Today, immigrants still move to the United States. They come to find better jobs and better lives.

GO ON.

Name _____ Date _____

PART 2: READING SELECTION #1

DIRECTIONS: For each question, circle the BEST answer. You may look back at the selection as often as necessary.

1 In paragraph 1, what does *settled* mean?

A. stayed away from

B. were happy about

C. often visited

D. made their homes

2 Which group of immigrants were LEAST interested in farming?

A. people from Scotland

B. people from Germany

C. people from China

D. people from Ireland

3 Which immigrants settled MOSTLY in Florida?

A. Russian

B. Cuban

C. Chinese

D. German

GO ON.

Name _____   Date _____

4 What made Swedish immigrants feel at home in Minnesota?

A. the people

B. the food

C. the weather

D. the neighborhoods

5 What is probably the BIGGEST hope of an immigrant?

A. to forget about home

B. to have a better life

C. to become world famous

D. to make new friends

GO ON.

Saturday Morning

1   Tory and Dad went to the farmer's market early every Saturday morning. There were always new things to see at the market.

2   First they stopped at the Italian bakery. Dad picked out bread, and Tory looked at the frosted cookies. Mr. Napoli smiled at Tory. He gave her a cookie. "I make these from my mother's old Italian recipe," he said. "It's a family tradition."

3   They went to the fruit stand next. "Ripe strawberries from South America!" Mr. Gonzalez said. His father owned a farm in Brazil. Dad bought some strawberries. Tori tasted one. It was sweet and juicy.

4   The Spice Man was next. Tory called him the Spice Man because he sold strange spices from around the world. He was from India. He wore a bright blue turban on his head. He winked at Tory as he wrapped spices in brown paper.

5 Finally, Dad and Tory went to the butcher, Mr. Deitrich. His family came from Germany. They had owned a butcher shop in Berlin many years ago. Mr. Deitrich showed Tory a photo of his grandfather's butcher shop. Then he gave her a <u>stick</u> of fresh beef jerky. "This is my secret recipe," he said. "I hope you like it!"

6 As Dad and Tory left the market, she thought about all the people there. They were from around the world. They had brought such good foods to America. She was glad.

GO ON.

Name _____ Date _____

PART 2: READING SELECTION #2

DIRECTIONS: For each question, circle the BEST answer. You may look back at the selection as often as necessary.

6 In paragraph 5, what does the word *stick* mean?

A. twig

B. piece

C. branch

D. bundle

7 In this story, Tory sees and talks to people who have relatives from

A. all over the world.

B. the nearby farms.

C. good restaurants.

D. the United States.

8 Which people use special recipes?

A. Mr. Napoli and Mr. Gonzalez

B. Mr. Napoli and Mr. Deitrich

C. Mr. Deitrich and Mr. Gonzalez

D. Mr. Gonzalez and the Spice Man

GO ON.

Name _____ Date _____

9 How does Tory probably feel on Saturday mornings?

A. tired

B. lonely

C. happy

D. bored

10 Look at the sequence of events from the story in the chart below.

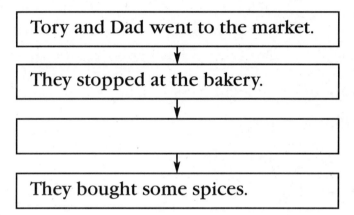

Which of these belongs in the empty box?

A. Tory got a piece of fresh beef jerky.

B. Tory and Dad left the market.

C. Dad picked out some bread.

D. Tory and Dad saw a photo of a butcher shop.

GO ON.

Name _____ Date _____

PART 2: CROSS-TEXT QUESTIONS

DIRECTIONS: Questions 11–12 ask about BOTH of the selections you read. For each question, circle the BEST answer. You may look back at the two selections as often as necessary.

11 Both selections have information about

A. railroads.

B. immigrants.

C. spices.

D. problems.

12 Which of these statements about the selections is TRUE?

A. One is an article, and the other is a story.

B. One is a biography, and the other is an article.

C. One is a story, and the other is a play.

D. One is a play, and the other is a biography.

STOP.

PART 2: WRITING IN RESPONSE TO READING

Tips for Using a Web

A web is a type of graphic organizer. You can use it to do some planning before you begin to write. It is a good tool when you want to gather information about a topic.

Below is an example of a web. It shows some information that Keesha collected. The information tells what people like about their pets. The center of the web is a square. In it is the main idea of her paragraph. There are five squares connected to the center square. These contain the information that Keesha will use to develop the main idea. These squares will be sentences in the paragraph.

Use a web to help you gather information. Then use the notes you make on the web when you do the first draft of your writing.

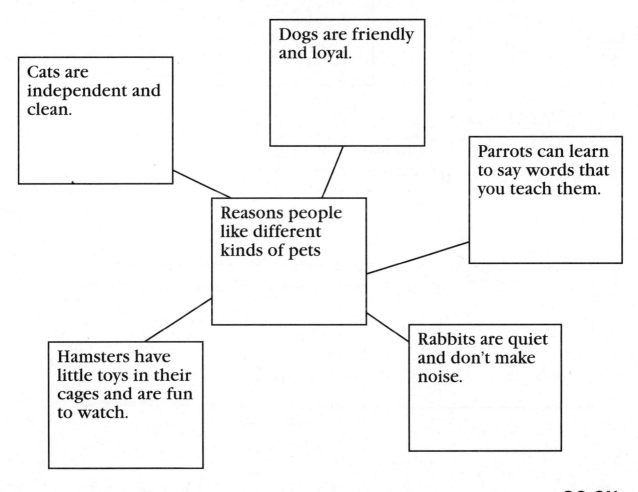

GO ON.

PART 2: WRITING IN RESPONSE TO READING

DIRECTIONS: Think about the information you learned in the selections you just read. Then answer the following question.

Do you think that the United States was settled by immigrants from many different places?

Think about the first selection. See if you can find some information about where immigrants came from. Use the squares to record what you find. Then think about the second selection. Do the same thing. Now read the information you have gathered on the web. Decide whether your answer to the question above is YES or NO. Then explain your answer by using specific examples and details from "Why They Came" and "Saturday Morning."

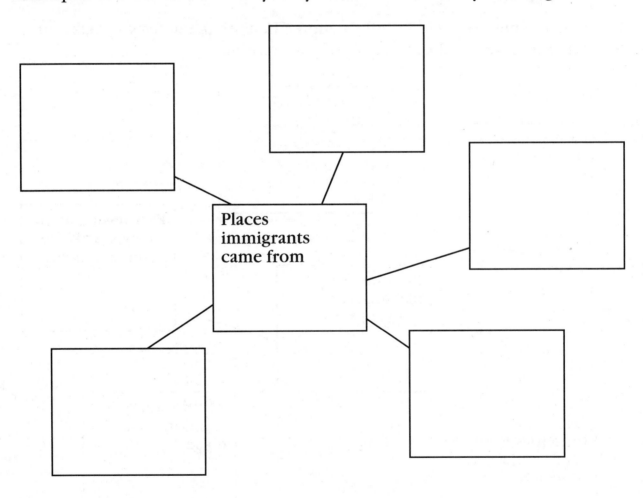

Places immigrants came from

GO ON.

MEAP Preparation and Practice **Level 2**

Name _____   Date _____

DRAFT

Remember to refer to the Revising and Editing Checklist on page 6 in this workbook as you develop your draft.

_____

_____

_____

_____

_____

_____

_____

_____

_____

_____

_____

_____

GO ON.

Name _____   Date _____

FINAL COPY

Use the English/Language Arts Rubric chart on pages 4 and 5 in this
workbook to check your writing and make changes.

_____

_____

_____

_____

_____

_____

_____

_____

_____

_____

_____

STOP.

PART 1: WRITING FROM KNOWLEDGE AND EXPERIENCE

This test is divided into two parts that are all linked to one theme or important idea. The theme for this unit is **Our Country and Its People.** Keep the theme in mind as you are taking this test.

In Part 1, you will be presented with a number of ways to write about the theme. You must choose ONLY ONE way. After you have finished reading the information provided, begin writing a draft. When you have completed your draft, use the REVISING AND EDITING CHECKLIST on page 6 in this workbook to review your writing. Then enter your final copy on the page marked FINAL COPY. You may use a dictionary, thesaurus, grammar book, or spelling book for Part 1 writing.

GO ON.

WRITE ABOUT THE THEME: Our Country and Its People

Our country has people who have come from all over the world. Some families have been in the United States for a long time. Other families have just arrived. When people come to the United States, they bring ideas about food, music, and entertainment. Some of the foods you eat, the music you hear, and the ways you have fun came from other countries. The new ideas and the older ideas make our country an interesting and exciting place to live.

Consider the following ideas for your piece of writing:
- Describe a game that you know began in another country.
- Tell about a time when you or someone you know went to a festival or party that celebrated the food and customs of another country.
- Tell about where your ancestors or the ancestors of someone you know came from.

You do not have to use the suggestions shown above. You can use your own idea about **Our Country and Its People** for your piece of writing. As you write about the theme, use examples from real life, from what you read or watch, or from your imagination.

Use a separate sheet of paper for listing ideas, organizing your thoughts, or writing a rough draft. You may use the REVISING AND EDITING CHECKLIST on page 6 in this workbook to help you as you work on your draft. When you are ready, you may begin your draft.

After you have finished your draft, you may use the English/Language Arts Rubric chart on pages 4 and 5 in this workbook to help you as you write your final copy.

GO ON.

Name _____   Date _____

FINAL COPY

Use the English/Language Arts Rubric chart on pages 4 and 5 in this workbook to check your writing and make changes.

_____

_____

_____

_____

_____

_____

_____

_____

_____

_____

_____

_____

STOP.

PART 2: READING

DIRECTIONS

Read Selection 1. Answer the five multiple-choice questions that follow Selection 1. You may look back at the selection at any time.

Go on to Selection 2. Answer the five multiple-choice questions that follow Selection 2. You may look back at the selection at any time.

Then answer the two multiple-choice questions in the section called PART 2: CROSS-TEXT QUESTIONS.

As you answer the multiple-choice questions, choose the BEST answer. Do not worry if there are questions you cannot answer. Take your time and do as well as you can.

When you have finished reading the selections and answering all of the questions, you may wish to go back and check your work. Do not go on to the next section until you are told to do so.

GO ON.

The Seminoles

1   The Seminole Indians are a proud people. Most Seminoles live in Florida. They have a colorful and exciting history.

2   The name *Seminole* comes from the word *Cimarron.* It means "wild men" or "runaway" in Spanish. Spanish explorers gave the Seminoles that name hundreds of years ago. At that time, the Seminoles were not one tribe. They were people from many different American Indian tribes. They moved to Florida to escape British colonists who treated them badly. These Native Americans joined together. They became known as the Seminoles.

3   The Seminoles hunted deer, turkey, and other game. They also fished in the waters of Florida. They were good farmers. They grew crops such as corn and a kind of banana. For many years, the Seminoles were successful.

4   In 1812 United States troops attacked the Seminoles. This started the Seminole War. Most Seminoles had to leave their homes. A few hid in the Everglades. After the war, the hidden people returned to their homes. Today most Seminoles in Florida are the descendants of those people. The Seminole Indians make up an important part of Florida's history.

GO ON.

Name _____   Date _____

PART 2: READING SELECTION #1

DIRECTIONS: For each question, circle the BEST answer. You may look back at the selection as often as necessary.

1 The Seminoles got their name from

A. British colonists.

B. Native Americans.

C. Spanish explorers.

D. Florida farmers.

2 The Seminoles came to Florida to escape

A. Native American tribes.

B. Spanish colonists.

C. British colonists.

D. Spanish runaways.

3 This story is mostly about

A. how a war started.

B. what the Seminoles ate.

C. where the first Seminoles came from.

D. a group of Native Americans called the Seminoles.

GO ON.

Name _____ Date _____

4 Look at the chain-of-events diagram.

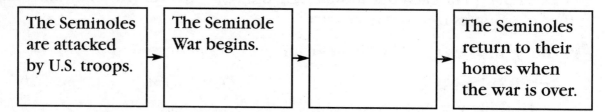

Which of these belongs in the empty box?

A. Many Seminoles leave their homes and go into hiding.

B. The Seminoles win the war.

C. Most Seminoles leave Florida.

D. The Seminoles escape from British colonists.

5 What kept some Seminoles safe during the war?

A. their warriors

B. hiding in the Everglades

C. their food supply

D. United States troops

GO ON.

Family Travels

1   Weekends at Aunt Jo's house were fun for LaTisha. Aunt Jo lived on the beach in Florida. LaTisha swam in the ocean. She played with her cousins, Bree and Daniel.

2   One day it rained. They couldn't play on the beach. Aunt Jo brought out a big box of family pictures. The children began looking at the <u>photographs</u>.

3   "Who is this?" LaTisha asked. She pointed to a picture of a man in a funny hat.

4   "That's your great-uncle Ralph," Aunt Jo said. "He lived in Chicago."

5   "Chicago!" Bree said. "How did he get all the way up there?"

Today, Grandpa lives in Florida and has his own fishing company.

---

6   Aunt Jo laughed. "We have family all over the country," she said.

7   Daniel looked at the pictures. "Why doesn't everyone live here in Florida, with us?" he asked.

8   "Well, most people traveled to find good jobs," Aunt Jo said. "Many years ago, our family lived in Alabama. But times were difficult. Ralph went to Chicago to find a job. He became a butcher. His brother, John, moved to New York City and became a newspaper reporter. Their sister, Jane, went all the way to California. She found work making costumes for the movies."

9   Aunt Jo smiled at the children. "Their little brother, Daniel, moved to Florida. He got a job on a fishing boat. Now he has his own fishing company. Do you know who he is today?"

10   "Grandpa!" they all yelled together.

GO ON.

Name _____   Date _____

PART 2: READING SELECTION #2

DIRECTIONS: For each question, circle the BEST answer. You may look back at the selection as often as necessary.

6 Aunt Jo gets out family pictures because she wants to

A. give the children something to do.

B. teach the children about their family's history.

C. explain why they live in Florida.

D. show the children how people used to dress.

7 What will the children probably do on the next sunny day at Aunt Jo's?

A. take pictures

B. go to the beach

C. go to work with their grandfather

D. sort the family pictures

8 In paragraph 2, what does the word *photographs* mean?

A. cards

B. CDs

C. books

D. pictures

GO ON.

Name _____ Date _____

9 Look at the chart about LaTisha's family.

Family Member	City or State	Job
Ralph	Chicago	Butcher
John	New York	Newspaper reporter
Jane		Costume maker
Daniel	Florida	Fisherman

Which of these belongs in the empty space?

A. Texas

B. Colorado

C. Alabama

D. California

10 Why did the family leave Alabama?

A. to visit friends

B. to live with cousins

C. to find work

D. to see the world

GO ON.

Name _____ Date _____

PART 2: CROSS-TEXT QUESTIONS

DIRECTIONS: Questions 11–12 ask about BOTH of the selections you read. For each question, circle the BEST answer. You may look back at the two selections as often as necessary.

11 Both selections have information about

A. Spanish explorers.

B. Chicago.

C. the Everglades.

D. Florida.

12 A title that might be good for both selections is

A. Hard Times.

B. The Photograph Box.

C. The First Immigrants.

D. On the Move.

STOP.

PART 2: WRITING IN RESPONSE TO READING

DIRECTIONS: Think about the information you learned in the selections you just read. Then answer the following question.

Do you think that the people mentioned in the selections moved from one place to another in the United States for the same reason?

Think about the first selection. Write down any notes that you think relate to the question above. Then think about the second selection. Again, write down notes that you think relate to the question. Read the notes that you have written. Decide whether your answer to the question above is YES or NO. Then explain your answer by using specific examples and details from "The Seminoles" and "Family Travels."

GO ON.

Name _____   Date _____

FINAL COPY

Use the English/Language Arts Rubric chart on pages 4 and 5 in your workbook to check your writing and make changes.

_____

_____

_____

_____

_____

_____

_____

_____

_____

_____

_____

_____

STOP.

_____